On the Riverfront, the gleaming Gateway Arch overlooking the Mississippi River rightly symbolizes the vital position St. Louis held in the westward expansion of the nation; and in Forest Park, proudly astride his charger, St. Louis rallies the city to continue its mission to the future.

Welcome to St. Louis!

INTRODUCTION

It has been our privilege to have shown St. Louis to a large number of stateside and foreign visitors, and in doing so we uncovered many of its best-kept secrets. The enthusiastic responses we received prepared and tested this guidebook and encouraged its publication to enhance your stay and make it memorable. St. Louis is indeed a good choice as a vacation area, for it is one of the most unique and diversified cities in America, not just for its location on the river, nor its heritage and charm, but due to the people, whose caring and vision have given St. Louis a special spirit.

A brief look at St. Louis' past has been included to acquaint you with some of the events, sites, and people who made this city the Gateway to the West, and to convey its animating pride and soul.

The river played a significant role in the development of St. Louis, and it was only after the area began to function as a city that the exploration of the West was made possible. Considering that St. Louis was founded 100 years later than the eastern cities, it boggles one's imagination to see how quickly St. Louis caught up with the rest of the country and the rest of the world, for only 150 years after humble beginnings, St. Louis was host to one of the most magnificent World's Fairs ever known. The small French village Pierre Laclede had settled near the confluence of the Mississippi and Missouri Rivers in 1764 was largely shaped by the traditions of the French, Spanish, German, and Irish immigrants and grew, as he had so well envisioned, into one of the finest and most successful cities of America, but remains a beautiful city with a relaxed and tolerant atmosphere.

There is something to appeal to everyone in the St. Louis vicinity: Museums; the Science Center; Zoo; Botanical Garden; Sports; Churches; Universities; Breweries; Wine Cellars; Ethnic Restaurants; Shopping Centers; Art Galleries; Theatres; and Indian Burial Grounds. Sightseeing Tours? And How! As a sample, you can visit historical areas, industries, neighborhoods, homes, national registry landmarks, and buildings of unique architectural interest. Area tours are available by boat, helicopter, bus, and foot. A large selection of night life awaits you: Dixieland and ragtime concerts; the Symphony; Broadway plays at the Fox Theatre and Muny Opera (an open-air theatre in Forest Park); dinner theatres; and all kinds of dancing to live music or D.J. productions. And for the children: the Zoo; the Magic House; the Dental Health Theatre; Six Flags Amusement Park; St. Louis Science Center; Kramer's Marionettes; and the Bearden Violin Shop are a few of the places that will delight and entertain.

Dennis A. Saunders   Jeanne-Marie Smith

ST. LOUIS IN YOUR POCKET

CONTENTS

THE RIVERFRONT

DOWNTOWN

SOUTH ST. LOUIS

SOUTH COUNTY

MIDTOWN

CENTRAL WEST END

5

EXCURSIONS

A BRIEF HISTORY OF ST. LOUIS

The Mississippi River played a major role in the development of St. Louis, the West, and the entire United States. It provided a route for the Indians and the earliest explorers, and encouraged them to settle in areas suited to their lifestyles. The Mississippians, believed to have come up the river about 1000 A.D., settled in St. Louis and Cahokia, IL [134] and left behind giant man-made hills. They were a highly civilized society, traders, and had many similarities with the Mayans of Mexico.

In 1500, Hernando de Soto, searching for gold, was the first European to sight the Mississippi. By the time the Spanish had come to explore Missouri, the Mississippians had totally disappeared, and the Missouri, Iowa, and Osage Indians lived on the land once inhabited by the Mound Builders. The Osage did not get along with the Spanish; to maintain peace, the Spanish had to trade horses and guns. This bargain was significant in that the horse, which had died out on the American continent during the Ice Age, was returned to the area. These new possessions led to many changes in the way the Indians lived.

The French were next to explore the River: Fr. Marquette and Louis Joliet, in 1673, discovered the Missouri River; and La Salle, in 1682, at the end of an expedition down the length of the Mississippi, called all the land drained by the Mississippi River "Louisiana Territory" and claimed it for the French King, Louis XIV. France's empire in the New World now stretched from the St. Lawrence River to New Orleans, and to protect their interests, the French began establishing trading posts.

In 1763, the New Orleans firm of Maxent, Laclede and Co. was commissioned by the King of France to set up a fur-trading post at the confluence of the Mississippi and Missouri rivers. Laclede, representing the firm and accompanied by 24 hired men, 7 of whom were Black, arrived several months later at Fort Chartres, IL, bringing the French settlers the news that France had recently ceded the east side of the Mississippi to the English. The French, not wishing to remain under English rule, began considering resettling with Laclede. In December, 1763, proceeding with his mission, Laclede singled out a site on the west bank of the Mississippi which he named St. Louis (after Louis IX, the patron Saint of Louis XV, the King of France), and, filled with dreams, returned to Fort Chartres and waited for Spring. On February 14, 1764, following Laclede's instructions, Auguste Chouteau, Laclede's fourteen-year old stepson, with the help of 30 men, began to build the new village. The original village stretched on the riverfront in the area now called the Jefferson National Expansion Memorial and Laclede's Landing [1-13]. When the village was finished, most of the French from Fort Chartres chose to resettle in St. Louis; however, some relocated in Ste. Genevieve, Portage des Sioux, and

St. Charles [106]. Two years later, the settlers learned that the Louisiana Territory had been given to Spain. Five years later, the Spanish Governor, Piernas, arrived at St. Louis to take command of the city. The French, however, were able to continue running their town without much interference from the Spanish who remained in St. Louis, until the Louisiana Territory was given back to France in 1800. In 1775, work began on the first Church west of the Mississippi [1]. In 1802, when the French presence became hostile to American interests, Thomas Jefferson offered to buy portions of the Louisiana Territory from France, and Napoleon, in 1803, agreed to sell the entire Louisiana Territory to the Americans for 15 million dollars. A sculpture by Karl Bittner at the Missouri Historical Society commemorates this event [63].

The first 20 years of the nineteenth century saw St. Louis' population swell with the arrival of pioneers from Kentucky, Tennessee, and North and South Carolina, and with the first wave of German, Irish, and Italian immigrants. By the same token, the city was now the "jumping off" point for adventurers heading for Oregon and the gold fields of California. The river traffic became so heavy by 1840 that several shipyards opened in the St. Louis area to repair the steamboats. Shortly after Missouri was called to statehood in 1820, a second, larger wave of European immigrants reached St. Louis, bringing their skills and their religious and ethnic cultures. By 1880, St. Louis could boast of 150,000 inhabitants. Many of these were well-educated entrepreneurs who became active in commerce and banking and became the leaders who shaped the city, the Midwest, and the nation. In 1818, the Jesuit Community founded St. Louis University [51] and construction was begun on the Courthouse in 1828 [13].

The 1840s were difficult years for St. Louis; a cholera epidemic claimed the lives of many of its citizens and floods and fires nearly leveled it. The city, however, bounced back, and rebuilt better than ever; and in 1853, William Greenleaf Elliott founded Washington University [79]. Before the outbreak of the Civil War, St. Louis was a significant commercial center, the first port on the Mississippi and the Gateway to the West. The Civil War, however, sharply divided St. Louisans, and abolitionists' activism, spurred by the Dred Scott case, made slavery a national issue. By 1868, Henry Shaw, an English immigrant who had made a fortune in the St. Louis hardware business, was determined to develop a Public Botanical Garden [39]. Before dying, he gave the 277 acres of the Botanical Garden and Tower Grove Park to the city. Shaw was aware of the ecological problems of the environment and had long envisioned the concept of residences in park-like settings. The beauty stemming from the tree-lined streets and plentiful parks of today is due in large measure to Shaw's influence. By 1874, the completion of Eads Bridge [5] and railroads across the country connected St. Louis to the rest of the nation and put stagecoaches and wagons out of business. In 1894, Union Station [28], the largest railroad station in the world, opened its doors.

The German immigrants used their knowledge of wine and beer to develop these industries in the St. Louis area [117][118]; Lemp's beer, the first German beer introduced in St. Louis, quickly replaced the English beer. The city, which at one time had 40 breweries, lost half of them in 1900 when Anheuser-Busch cornered a national market with advertising and the introduction of pasteurized bottled beer.

By 1887, St. Louis counted 100 millionaires. These powerful men were influential not only in St. Louis, but throughout the nation. They lived in exclusive neighborhoods with ornate gates which closed out public traffic. These residential enclaves, referred to as "Private Places", are to this day showcases of elegance exemplifying all types of architecture. Some such "places" are Westmoreland, Portland, Kingsbury, Central West End [70], and Compton Heights [58]. St. Louis innovated the concept of the private places, the precursors of the nation's suburbs.

The 1904 World's Fair, which commemorated the Centennial of the Louisiana Purchase, brought St. Louis to the world's attention. The Fair in Forest Park [62] lasted 7 months and its success was a boost to the city. The Olympic Games held during the Fair had been the very first ones held in America. The Art Museum [66] is one of the buildings which was not demolished after the Fair. The bird cage at the Zoo [67] was purchased from the Smithsonian Institute's Bird Exhibit and Francis Field [79], which hosted the Olympic Games during the Fair, was kept at Washington University. The statue, "The Apotheosis of St. Louis" [66], originally sculpted for the Fair, was recast in bronze and placed in front of the Art Museum. Spurred by the successes of the Fair and the sense of renewal it brought the city, the Zoo [67], the Muny Opera [65], and the Missouri Historical Society [63] were opened in the Park. The city kept growing. The New Cathedral on Lindell [59] was completed in 1914, and its superb mosaics in 1985.

St. Louis was a pioneer in the automobile industry; in 1922 there were 115,000 cars in St. Louis, now the Chevrolet, Chrysler, and Ford Assembly plants produce that many in just 3 months.

Lindbergh's famous non-stop transatlantic flight in 1927 called attention to St. Louis as an aviation center. The city took great strides in the aviation and space industry. Mercury, the capsule which sent the first American, John Glenn, into space was the first of many such capsules to be made by the McDonnell Douglas Company of St. Louis [93].

The St. Louis Baseball Cardinals won the World's Championship in 1926, 1931, 1934, 1942, 1944, 1946, 1964, 1967, and 1982. The St. Louis Blues Hockey Team and the St. Louis Storm Indoor Soccer Team draw over 700,000 fans per year to the St. Louis Arena (Plans are now afoot for these teams to move to an enlarged

Kiel Auditorium in the near future). The development of the Jefferson National Expansion Memorial in the 1960s revitalized the Riverfront and spurred a renewal throughout the whole city. The St. Louis area is a cultural and educational center which boasts 2 of the best medical schools in the country, 4 universities which have produced more than 15 Nobel Laureates, some of the best hospitals in the country, and 24 colleges. The French, Spanish, Irish, and Germans were the main European immigrants who helped shape the early character of the city. With the exception of the Italian community on the Hill [40], evidence of the original neighborhoods is no longer as visible as it once was; however, people from more than 40 countries have enriched the St. Louis area and have benefitted by what they have found here.

Your visit in St. Louis has been organized by areas and will take you to Downtown, South St. Louis, the Hill, South County, Midtown, Central West End, Clayton, West County, North County, North St. Louis, and the immediate neighboring areas.

Areas To Visit

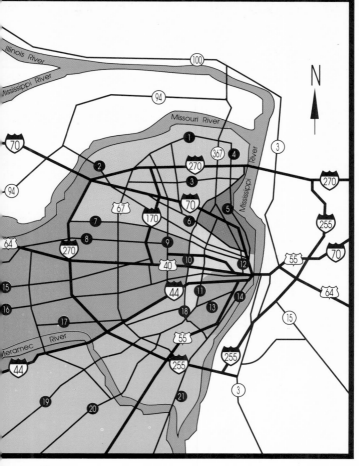

● STREET
1 Lindbergh
2 St. Charles Rk. Rd.
3 Chambers
4 Bellefontaine
5 Riverview
6 Natural Bridge Rd.
7 Page Blvd.

8 Olive Blvd.
9 Hanley Rd.
10 Goodfellow
11 Kingshighway
12 Tucker Blvd.
13 Grand Blvd.
14 Broadway
15 Clayton Rd.

16 Manchester
17 Big Bend Rd.
18 Hampton
19 Gravois
20 Tesson Ferry Rd.
21 Telegraph Rd.

Downtown

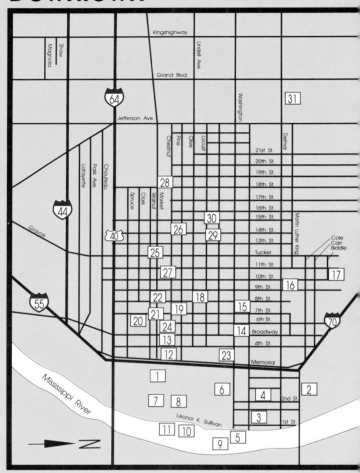

POINTS OF INTEREST
1 Old Cathedral
2 Laclede's Landing
3 Dental Health Theater
4 Laclede's Landing Wax Museum
5 Eads Bridge
6 Gateway Arch Grounds
7 The Gateway Arch
8 Museum of Westward Expansion
9 Gateway Riverboat Cruises
10 Fostaire Heliport
11 U.S.S. Inaugural No. 242
12 Luther Ely Smith Park
13 Old Courthouse
14 The Forum
15 Mercantile Money Museum
16 Cervantes Convention Center
17 Shrine of St. Joseph
18 Old Post Office
19 Wainwright Building
20 Busch Memorial Stadium
21 St. Louis Sports Hall of Fame
22 National Bowling Hall of Fame
23 St. Louis Visitors Center
24 Kiener Plaza
25 City Hall
26 Soldiers' Memorial Military Museum
27 Serra Sculpture
28 St. Louis Union Station
29 Christ Church Cathedral
30 Campbell House Museum
31 Scott Joplin House

THE RIVERFRONT
The Jefferson National Expansion Memorial

Pierre Laclede would undoubtedly be stunned to see what has become of the riverfront! The Jefferson National Expansion Memorial, established to honor Thomas Jefferson and his clever purchase of the Louisiana Territory and to give tribute to all those who opened the West, occupies the site upon which Laclede settled his small village of St. Louis more than 225 years ago. This project, begun in 1935, ignited an urban renewal which not only revitalized the riverfront but the entire city. The Jefferson National Expansion Memorial encompasses the Old Cathedral, the Gateway Arch Grounds, the Gateway Arch, the Riverfront, the Luther Ely Smith Park, and the Old Courthouse.

1 THE OLD CATHEDRAL —
THE BASILICA OF SAINT LOUIS, KING OF FRANCE
209 Walnut St, 63102; (314) 231-3250.
Cathedral and Museum open daily; Cathedral, 6am-6pm; Museum, 10am-4:30pm. Daily Masses. Free admission and parking. Museum entrance on west side; small admission fee.

Designated a National Monument by President Kennedy, the Old Cathedral stands on the original parcel of land Laclede had set aside for the Church and cemetery of his village; this is the only parcel of land in St. Louis which has not been purchased or sold. His log Chapel was to be the first Church built in St. Louis and has since been replaced 3 times. In 1818, it received the title of Cathedral, the first west of the Mississippi. The present Cathedral, of Greek Revival style*, was completed in 1834. Pope John XXIII proclaimed it a Basilica in 1961. At the entrance, a brief recording of the Church's history can be heard by pushing a button on the wall. Group tours can be arranged, and an upstairs Museum displays interesting historical documents on early St. Louis and Catholics of the area.

* The Greek Revival architecture, so popular in St. Louis and in America between 1820 and 1840, has erroneously been named. The style was not a revival, but the birth of a new American architecture which borrowed from the Greeks at a time when Americans were sympathetic to the Greek struggle for independence (1821-1829). This kindred spirit also manifested itself in other aspects of American life, especially in the Greek names Americans were giving their towns.

2 LACLEDE'S LANDING
Between the Eads and Martin Luther King Bridges; (314) 241-5875, Laclede's Landing Merchants Association.

Laclede's Landing is the only section left of the original grid pattern of cobblestone streets which French settlers used as they built St. Louis. The original names of the three main streets running parrallel to the Mississippi River, Rue Royale, Rue de l'Eglise, and Rue des Granges, were renamed to First, Second, and Third Streets. Plaques in Laclede's Landing mark interesting historical sites. In 1804, as St. Louis was becoming a bustling commercial center for the railroads and steamboats, the original houses of the early settlers were razed to build warehouses close to the levee. With the advent of the automobile, the narrow streets soon made the area obsolete. In 1969, private concerns rescued the area from its decaying state and rehabilitated the beautiful original brick buildings with ornamental cast iron fronts into an exciting hospitality district with shops, restaurants, nightclubs, and lounges. Laclede's Landing, with its gaslight lamps and cobblestone streets, offers a very quaint taste of St. Louis' past.

3 DENTAL HEALTH THEATRE

727 N. First St, Suite 103, Laclede's Landing, 63102; (314) 241-7391. Open year round, M-F, 9am-4pm. Reservations are required for groups of 10 or more. Call for show times. Free admission.

The only theatre in the world combining entertainment and dental health education. The theatre stage consists of 16 three-feet high teeth which light up. There are also movies and a marionette show.

4 LACLEDE'S LANDING WAX MUSEUM

720 N. Second St, Laclede's Landing, 63102; (314) 241-1155. Open daily, 10am-10pm. Admission fee.

Located in Laclede's Landing, this Wax Museum of 180 life-like wax figures of Kings, Queens, Presidents, movie stars, world leaders, scientists, and...monsters dressed in authentic costumes provides an interesting visit.

5 THE EADS BRIDGE

Recognized as an engineering marvel, this graceful bridge was the world's first truss bridge and the first railroad bridge to span the Mississippi. Its construction on stone piers stirred much controversy among engineers all over the world, for all contended it could not endure the strong current of the river. James Eads, however, inventing some of the needed equipment and using pneumatic underwater methods he had learned in Europe, made the construction possible. It took 7 years and 10 million dollars to build the bridge, but its completion in 1874 connected St. Louis to the Atlantic and the Pacific by rail and made Union Station [28] one of the largest railroad centers in the world.

6 THE GATEWAY ARCH GROUNDS

Consisting of 91 acres of manicured lawns and trees surrounding the Gateway Arch, this almost-always breezy spot offers an excellent view of the Mississippi River.

7 | THE GATEWAY ARCH

(Jefferson National Expansion Memorial, National Park) 11 N. 4th St, 63102; (314) 425-4465. Open daily, 8am-10pm, Memorial Day through Labor Day; 9am-6pm rest of year, except Thanksgiving, Dec 25, and Jan 1. Admission fee for tram rides. The access from L.K. Sullivan Blvd, the riverfront, has many stairs. To avoid steps: take elevator to the top floor of the Arch parking lot and step into the Park area.

Designed by Eero Saarinen, a Finnish architect, the Arch construction began in 1962 and was completed in 1965. Soaring 630 feet above the river, the Gateway Arch is the tallest of America's great National Monuments, an engineering masterpiece, and a symbol of St. Louis' role in the westward expansion and America's progress. A tram ride to the top of the graceful catenary curve of the Arch offers a panoramic view of 30 miles' radius.

8 | THE MUSEUM OF WESTWARD EXPANSION

Open daily, 8am-10pm, Memorial Day through Labor Day; 9am-6pm rest of year. Small admission fee.

Located under the Arch, the Museum has exhibits and guided tours focusing on Indians, the early settlers in Missouri, and the Oregon and Santa Fe Trails departing from Missouri.
- The Tucker Theater features a film explaining the innovative construction of the Arch. Small admission fee.
- A Tourist Information Booth can be found in the center.

9 | GATEWAY RIVERBOAT CRUISES

500 L.K. Sullivan Blvd, 63102; (314) 621-4040 or (800) 878-7411. Tours daily, 10am-5pm, Apr 1-Dec 1. Admission fee.

Operated by the oldest river excursion company on the Mississippi, the Huck Finn, the Tom Sawyer, and the Becky Thatcher offer 1-hour narrated cruises of the historic St. Louis Riverfront with frequent departures every day, Mar 1-Jan 1. Dinner Dixieland cruises, too! Below the Arch, the Belle of St. Louis, St. Louis' newest cruising riverboat, offers a 2-hour day trip, T-Su, and Moonlight Dinner Cruises, W-Su. A wide variety of entertainment on board, live music, and great reviews. Fun for the whole family.

10 | FOSTAIRE HELIPORT

400 L.K. Sullivan Blvd, 63102; (314) 421-5440.
Flights daily, 10am-dusk, mid-Apr through Oct, depending on weather conditions; 421-3388 for information regarding tours.

An FAA-approved heliport moored on the levee offers tours of varying lengths. Excellent for photography, a quick and wonderful way to see the city.

11 U.S.S. INAUGURAL No. 242

400 L.K. Sullivan Blvd, 63102; (314) 771-9911. Open daily, 10am-dusk, Apr 1 through Nov 1, weather permitting. Visit and tour at your leisure. Personal tours available upon request. Small admission fee; children under 5 free with an adult.

This World War II U.S. Navy Minesweeper from the Battle of Okinawa is a National Historic Landmark.

12 LUTHER ELY SMITH PARK

4th St to Memorial Dr, Chestnut to Market St.

Situated in front of the Old Courthouse, the park is a memorial to Luther Ely Smith, a St. Louis attorney who, in 1933, was the person most responsible for the riverfront rehabilitation and for making the Jefferson National Expansion Memorial a reality.

13 THE OLD COURTHOUSE

Broadway and Chestnut St, 63102; (314) 425-4465. Open daily, 8am-4:30pm except Thanksgiving, Dec 25, and Jan 1. Free admission. Wheelchair accessible.

The land for the Courthouse was donated by Auguste Chouteau and J.B. Lucas with a stipulation that it only be used as the site of a Courthouse. The first Courthouse, built in 1828, started as a small building and as population increased, the building of Greek Revival style was gracefully enlarged and was completed in 1862. Beautiful paintings by Carl Wimar adorning the Rotunda's ceiling depict historical scenes. The iron dome designed by William Rumbold and the one designed by Thomas Walter for the Capitol in Washington were the first of their kind in the U.S. and became prototypes for many others. The Courthouse served to settle the legal battles over fur trading, the railroad, slavery, and equal rights. It also was a place to debate the important issues of the day; on its eastern steps, slaves were auctioned. In 1847, Dred Scott, a St. Louis slave, sued for his freedom at the Courthouse, claiming that having lived in free territory released him from slavery. This case stirred the conscience of the land and was partially responsible for the Civil War and slavery's ultimate abolishment. All courts moved from the Courthouse to the new Civil Courts Building in 1930, and the City of St. Louis deeded the Old Courthouse to the National Park Service in 1940.

DOWNTOWN

14 THE FORUM

555 Washington Ave, 63101; (314) 421-3791. M-F, 11am-6pm. Free admission. Wheelchair accessible. Evening performances. Call for week-end schedules.

This visual and performing arts center features 5 visual exhibitions a year and several performances. The Forum also presents exhibitions of paintings, sculptures, and ceramics, which address contemporary and historical issues.

15 MERCANTILE MONEY MUSEUM

7th and Washington, Mercantile Tower Building, Podium level (connected to the St. Louis Centre by skywalk), 63101; (314) 421-1819, group visit reservations: 425-8199. Open 7 days a week, 9am-4pm. Free Admission. Allow 30-60 minutes.

The Mercantile Money Museum was founded by Eric P. Newman, an international authority on numismatics. The exhibits are so well researched and presented that visitors will learn in less than an hour more about the history of money in America than in any course they could take. Exhibits show money used in the country prior to our own federal minting and the role Benjamin Franklin played in the development and printing of American money. Learn how to recognize counterfeit money, browse over national and foreign gold coins, see Missouri's own paper money, $3 bills, and learn about the interrelationship of money with Indians, Blacks, and Women.

16 CERVANTES CONVENTION CENTER

801 Convention Plaza, 63101; (314) 342-5000 or 342-5036. Offices open weekdays, 8am-5pm. Call for show hours. Convention Center open during events.

The Cervantes Convention Center hosts many national exhibitions, shows, and conventions in its 3 major exhibit halls. Now expanding, additional exhibit and meeting space is being added. Call for information and schedules.

17 THE SHRINE OF ST. JOSEPH

1120 N. 11th St, 63106; (314) 231-9407. Tours by appointment, daily, 9am-3pm, or after 11am Mass on Su, all year.

Built in 1844 by the Jesuits, the Shrine was expanded in 1866 to its present Baroque architecture, and is the only Baroque Church remaining in St. Louis. It has been honored in the National Register of Historic Places. It has a beautiful Altar of Answered Prayers, a monument donated to St. Joseph by grateful parishioners whose lives had been spared during the St. Louis cholera epidemic of 1866. The Church boasts of a well-documented miracle involving a German immigrant, a parishioner, who recovered from a seemingly incurable illness. The Church houses a relic of St. Peter Claver and one of the largest Pfeffer tracker organs in existence. The Shrine, doomed to be destroyed for urban renewal, was spared and the restoration which began in 1980 was 95% complete as of Dec, 1990.

18 THE OLD POST OFFICE
815 Olive, 63101; (314) 621-0044, Open M-S, 9am-5pm. Closed Su.
Completed in 1884 and restored in 1982 to its original beauty and elegance, the structure is now occupied by a small post office, a mall, federal offices, an art gallery, and private commercial shops. A skylight accentuates the space of this unusual structure.

19 THE WAINWRIGHT BUILDING
7th and Chestnut Sts, 63101; (314) 444-6800. Parking across street. Visit on your own or call for tour schedules.
A work of modern art well worth seeing; the Wainwright Building, elegantly restored to new life in 1979, now holds offices for 700 state employees. Built in 1891 by architect Louis Sullivan, the Wainwright Building, prototype of all skyscrapers, and now more handsome than ever, revolutionized American architecture. Its restoration has been enhanced by the perceptive and balanced use of the old and new, colors and lights. The central feature of the renovated building is the spectacular glass atrium which in itself brings life and light to the already spacious and airy interior. Shallow pools of water and interesting water channels circulate around the building, creating an island of silence away from the noise of the city. Terra cotta relief ornaments, works of art in themselves, border the bases of windows with different designs for each floor.

20 BUSCH MEMORIAL STADIUM
Walnut to Spruce, Broadway to 7th St, 63102; (314) 421-3060. Admission fee.
With seating for over 50,000 fans of the St. Louis Cardinals Baseball Team, this beautiful arena is recognized as one of the most attractive in the country. This anchor of downtown renewal also hosts circuses, concerts, and high school and college sporting events. A restaurant, the Hall of Fame Club, a gift shop, and two garages are also available.

21 ST. LOUIS SPORTS HALL OF FAME
100 Stadium Plaza (in Busch Memorial Stadium), 63102; (314) 421-FAME. Mar through Dec, 10am-5pm, until 11pm on nights of ballgames; Jan through Feb, call for hours. Admission fee. Reservation required for groups of 15 or more. Buy ticket for self-guided Museum tour or a combination ticket for the Museum and the

conducted Busch Stadium tour.

This Museum is the repository for St. Louis sports history, records, trophies, and memorabilia. Many sports are represented: Baseball, Football, Basketball, Golf, Soccer, Hockey, and Olympic events. The Museum tours are self-conducted; the conducted Stadium tours give the visitor a chance to see behind the scenes of the games; see the stadium, learn about the Cardinals, see the Press Box area, the Cardinal dugout, and...much more.

22 NATIONAL BOWLING HALL OF FAME AND MUSEUM
111 Stadium Plaza, 63102; (314) 231-6340. Memorial Day through Labor Day; M-S, 9am-7pm; Su, Noon-7pm; rest of year, M-F, 9am-5pm; Su, Noon-5pm. Closed Thanksgiving, Dec 24, 25, 31, and Jan 1. Admission fee. Wheelchair accessible.

This Museum is the only Bowling Museum in the world. A movie introduces the visitor to the origin of bowling, the variations throughout the world, its heroes, and the social, political, religious, and recreational roles it has had in the Western world. Many photographs, paintings, and unusual memorabilia back up the newly-acquired knowledge. The visitor can hear what famous bowlers have to say about their careers and also play a game on the Oldtime Alleys or modern computerized lanes (for a minimal fee, which includes balls and shoes). Relax for a while at Cafe 300. A gift shop is available. Don't miss seeing the 240-year old Aubusson tapestry depicting "A Dutchman Lawn-Bowling", and the world's only bowling pin car.

23 ST. LOUIS VISITORS CENTER
308 Washington Ave at Memorial Dr, 63102; (314) 241-1764. Open everyday, 9:30am-4:30pm, except Thanksgiving, Dec 25, and Jan 1.

Volunteers welcome visitors and help enhance a visit to St. Louis. The Visitors Center offers: complete information on St. Louis; free brochures, maps, and pamphlets; tour guides; and attractive gifts with a St. Louis flavor. There is also a Speakers Bureau for Slide Presentations available.

24 KIENER PLAZA
Broadway to 7th, Market to Chestnut.

The beautiful fountains and the sculpture of the "Olympic Runner" on Kiener Plaza, graceful focal points in this popular downtown area, were made possible by Henry J. Kiener's bequest specifying a fountain with an athletic figure. The fountains were the work of Eugene Mackey and the sculpture that of William Zorach, who chose to pay tribute to Henry J. Kiener's love for the sport of running and his participation on the 1904 Olympic track team.

25 CITY HALL

1203 Market St, 63101; (314) 622-4000. Open to public M-F, 8am-5pm all year except holidays.

Located at the corner of Tucker Blvd and Market St, this imposing structure is modeled after the Hotel de Ville of Paris (Paris City Hall). The building of Missouri pink granite and sandstone is guarded by two statues, General Ulysses Grant on Tucker Blvd (sculpted by St. Louis' first professional sculptor, Robert Bringhurst) and Pierre Laclede (by Julian Zolnay), the city's founder, on Market St. The structure, completed in 1904, has a very sumptuous interior. The walls; the floors; the white marble grand staircase; the impressive stained glass atrium framed with plaster moldings; frescos depicting scenes of Indians and settlers painted by Frederick Lincoln Stoddard in the spandrels between the arches; all speak to the grandeur. A perfect setting for a formal Ball; in fact, several such galas are held in the lobby each year.

26 SOLDIERS' MEMORIAL MILITARY MUSEUM

1315 Chestnut, 63103; (314) 622-4550. Open daily, 9am-4:30pm; Free admission. Closed Thanksgiving, Dec 25, and Jan 1.

This memorial, located across Market St from the Municipal Courts Building, was dedicated by President Roosevelt in 1936 to the 1,075 St. Louisans who died in action in World War I and whose names are listed on the black granite cenotaph. Another Memorial, "The Court of Honor", across Chestnut St, was added later to honor the St. Louisans who died in World War II, Korea, and Vietnam. The Museum contains photographs and memorabilia pertaining to St. Louisans' military involvement since the Civil War. Other features of interest are: the colorful mosaic ceiling of the loggia, above the cenotaph, dedicated to the mothers of St. Louisans who died in wars; and the 4 massive Bedford Stone sculptures (the work of St. Louis artist Walker Hancock) depicting Courage, Sacrifice, Vision, and Loyalty, which guard the entrances of the Memorial Building.

27 THE SERRA SCULPTURE

Serra Sculpture Park, Market to Chestnut, 10th to 11th, 63103.

This 1981 rusted, wall-like sculpture titled "Twain", is the work of Richard Serra, a renowned modern Spanish artist who uses rusted industrial steel to symbolize his solidarity with the working class. This innovative environmental sculpture, one of the most controversial in St. Louis, was designed not to draw attention to itself, but rather to the cityscape. Although the total sculpture is best seen from above, the way to experience what the artist intends it to do is to stand in the center of the enclave it creates and focus one's attention upon the city scenes the structure frames above its walls and through its openings. The sculpture also provides within the noisy city a space for thoughts in solitude.

28 ST. LOUIS UNION STATION

1820 Market St, 63103; (314) 421-6655. Open M-Th, 10am-9pm; F-S, 10am-10pm; Su, 10am-6pm.

Theodore C. Link was the architect who won the contest initiated in March, 1881, which had invited 10 prominent architects to submit drawings for the Union Station. His elegant, castle-like rendition was inspired by the walled city of Carcasonne in the South of France. Under construction for 14 months, the station opened its doors in 1894 with an impressive ceremony in the magnificent Grand Hall. Union Station was unique in that people could change trains within the same station. The largest station in the world soon made St. Louis a convention center and was the scene of much congested traffic during the World Wars. Airplane travel eventually caused Union Station to be closed; however, in 1985, it was elegantly restored to the glory of its past and is today a very interesting mix-use center. St. Louis Union Station Memory Theater offers the history of the station as told through the eyes of a pullman conductor, the story of the rebirth of the station, and the story of railroads in America. Group tours of Union Station should be booked months ahead by writing to: The Rouse Co of Missouri, 500 St. Louis Union Station, St. Louis, MO, 63103. Facing Union Station, on Aloe Plaza, the beautiful "Meeting of the Waters" fountain jets its waters into the air. Its 14 bronze figures, designed and sculpted by Carl Milles, remind us how Laclede selected the site for his city at the confluence of the Mississippi and Missouri Rivers.

29 CHRIST CHURCH CATHEDRAL

13th and Locust Sts, 63103; (314) 231-3454, M-F, 9am-4pm; S, closed; Su, 7:30am-1pm.

A Gothic structure built during the Civil War features a sizable stone altar screen inspired by the St. Albans Abbey and Winchester altar screens in England. The screen was carved by Harry Hems, of Exeter, England, and took 11 months to be completed.

30 THE CAMPBELL HOUSE MUSEUM

1508 Locust St, 63103; (314) 421-0325. Open Mar 1-Dec 31; T-S, 10am-4pm; Su, Noon-5pm. Small admission fee. Group rates available. Gift Shop.

The Campbell House Museum, an 1851 Victorian townhouse in downtown St. Louis, is the sole survivor of Lucas Place. This neighborhood, once on the outskirts of the city, was where the elite of St. Louis resided prior to and following the Civil War. The mansion contains original furnishings, china, and memorabilia belonging to the Robert Campbell family and is currently being restored to reflect the Victorian styles of Robert and Virginia's day. Col. Robert Campbell made his early connections and fortune in the Rocky Mountain Fur Company and worked with such legends as Kit Carson, Jim Bridger, Jedidiah Smith , and Thomas Fitzpatrick. He was a trusted and respected friend of both the White men and the Indian tribes of the west. His home was the setting for dinner parties and balls for President and Mrs. Grant, Father DeSmet, and General Sherman. Of their 13 children, 3 survived the senior Campbells and continued to occupy this home into the early 20th century.

31 THE SCOTT JOPLIN HOUSE STATE HISTORIC SITE
2658 Delmar Blvd, 63103; (314) 533-1003.

The Scott Joplin House State Historic Site was designated a National Historic Landmark in 1976 and became a state-owned historic site in 1984. From 1900 to 1903, Scott Joplin, the King of Ragtime, lived with his young bride at this address. Having successfully published "The Maple Leaf Rag", he was able to settle down in St. Louis, abandoning forever the itinerant pianist lifestyle of his ragtime pioneering days in St. Louis, Nashville, New Orleans, Chicago, and on riverboats. It was at this address that he composed "The Cascades", a tribute to the 1904 St. Louis World's Fair, "The Entertainer", "Elite Syncopation", "March Majestic", and many other works. Recently restored, the house offers an insight into Joplin's life, talent, and the popularity of his music at the turn of the century: a man ahead of his time. A room features musical performances, and a gallery displays exhibits relating to Black history and culture. The Friends of the Scott Joplin House sponsor a Ragtime Rendez-vous, the second week-end in Jun.

8

9

10

11

12

outh St. Louis

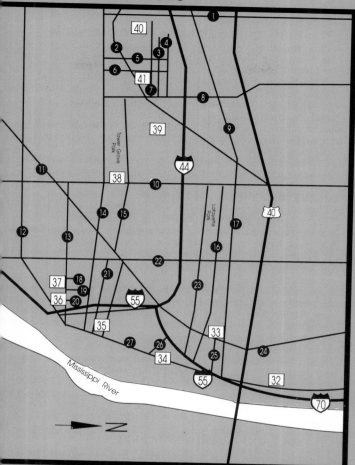

POINTS OF INTEREST
32 Eugene Field House and Toy Museum
33 St. Raymond's Maronite Church
34 Soulard Farmer's Market
35 Anheuser-Busch Brewery
36 Chatillon-De Menil Mansion
37 Lemp Mansion
38 Tower Grove Park
39 Missouri Botanical Garden
40 The Hill
41 St. Ambrose Church

● STREET
1 Hampton Ave.
2 Southwest
3 Daggett
4 Shaw
5 Edwards
6 Marconi
7 Wilson
8 Kingshighway
9 Manchester
10 Grand Ave.
11 Gravois
12 Chippewa
13 Cherokee

14 Arsenal
15 Magnolia
16 Park
17 Chouteau
18 Lemp
19 18th
20 De Menil
21 Pestalozzi
22 Jefferson
23 Lafayette
24 Tucker
25 Lebanon
26 Soulard
27 Broadway

SOUTH ST. LOUIS

32 EUGENE FIELD HOUSE AND TOY MUSEUM
634 S. Broadway, 63102; (314) 421-4689. Open T-S, 10am-4pm; Su, Noon-4pm. Admission fee. Free parking. Not recommended for pre-school children.

This National Landmark home (1845) was the birthplace of Eugene Field (1850-1895), America's Children's poet, best known for "The Sugar Plum Tree", and "Wynken, Blynken, and Nod", which he wrote while a journalist for the Chicago Daily News. His father, Roswell Field, is best remembered as the lawyer for Dred Scott. The house is an historic house museum, featuring a large collection of antique toys and dolls, as well as original furnishings, and memorabilia from Field's adult years. The gift shop sells dolls, reproductions of antique toys, and books of Field's poetry.

33 ST. RAYMOND'S MARONITE CHURCH
931 Lebanon Dr, 63104; (314) 621-0056. Open M-F, 8:30am-4pm; Su, 8:30am-2pm. Lebanese lunches W, Noon-4pm.

At the turn of the century, Lebanese Christians, persecuted by Moslems, began immigrating to the United States; many settled in St. Louis, and in 1898, built a church which became the center of the Lebanese Community. In 1975, the need for a larger Church became evident. The construction of the new St. Raymond's Church became the catalyst of the Lasalle Park redevelopment, an area which was decaying. Though St. Raymond's parishioners are now scattered throughout the metropolitan area, the Church has remained the center of the community. The Church has a large golden dome in Eastern style architecture, and stained glass windows depicting the story of the Lebanese exodus to America and flight from persecution. The low wall surrounding the Church symbolizes the mountains behind which they found safety, and in the court yard, one can find the only two Lebanese Cedar trees in St. Louis. Services are conducted in Aramaic, the language Christ spoke on earth, and an outstanding choir can be heard on Su and holidays.

34 SOULARD FARMER'S MARKET
1601 S. 7th St, 63104; (314) 622-4180.
Indoor market: T-F, 8am-5:30pm; S, 6am-5:30pm. Outdoor market: open everyday, 7am-6:30pm Flea Market: May-Oct, 1st Su of month, 8am-4pm.

Located just a few miles south of the Arch, the market has been in operation for over 211 years. Local farmers bring their produce and supply the city and most restaurants. The market sheds and Community Center were renovated in 1929 in the Italian Renaissance style. The land, once a fruit orchard owned by the Soulards, was donated to the city in 1842. The neighborhood (also called Soulard) is an area of many ethnic groups and Churches.

35 ANHEUSER-BUSCH BREWERY

13th and Lynch, 63118; (314) 577-2626. No reservation needed for tours. Complimentary tour (about 8 blocks); M-S every 10 minutes, 9am-4pm. Allow 1½ hours. Children must be accompanied by adults.

Here is a chance to see the world's largest brewery in action in all its phases: beer brewing in large shining copper vats; bottling; packaging; sampling the products; and seeing the Clydesdales, horses which once pulled beer delivery trucks in the city. The company originated in St. Louis and is today one of 12 plants throughout the country. The Clydesdale 8-horse hitch has become a symbol of the Anheuser-Busch Brewery and is frequently seen in festivals and parades at home and overseas.

36 THE CHATILLON-DE MENIL MANSION

3352 DeMenil Pl, 63118; (314) 771-5828.
Open T-S, 10am-4pm. Closed Jan. Small admission fee.

The first building on this site overlooking the Mississippi River was built in 1849 by Henry Chatillon, a trapper with the American Fur Co, who had been a guide for Francis Parkman's journey depicted in *The Oregon Trail*. The house was later sold to Dr. DeMenil, who added several rooms and the Greek Revival porch columns and wrought iron grilles on the windows. The house features furnishings from the mid-Victorian period (1850-1870), and the Carriage House Restaurant is adjacent to the building. There is also a Museum Shop in the Mansion.

37 THE LEMP MANSION

3322 DeMenil Pl; 63118; (314) 664-8024.

The Lemp Mansion, residence of the Lemp family, the first to introduce German beer in St. Louis under the name of Falstaff Beer, was restored in 1960, and is now used as an elegant restaurant with the atmosphere of the 1880s. The Lemp's brewery buildings still stand in the nearby area and are a reminder of an era gone by. In 1980, the Lemp Mansion received national attention in a *Life* magazine article which listed it as one of the 9 most haunted houses in America. Bizarre incidents reported in this Mansion, once the site of much drama and 3 family suicides, have always been explained as harmless pranks played on people living or working in the house. Guests are invited to browse through the house.

38 TOWER GROVE PARK

Grand to Kingshighway, Arsenal to Magnolia; (314) 771-2679. Cycles available (fee) Jun through Aug, T-Su, Noon-dusk; Apr, May, Sept, Oct, S and Su, Noon-dusk. Full tennis facilities, Stupp

Senior Center, ballfields, and weekly concerts.

One of the most beautiful parks in St. Louis was donated to the city by Henry Shaw, who planted 10,000 trees, covering 200 varieties. The park, which is now a National Historic Landmark, is graced with gazebos, statues, and a Fountain Pond complete with water lillies and mid-19th century mock ruins. Relive the past and spend an hour cycling, picnicking, or strolling through this beautiful Victorian park.

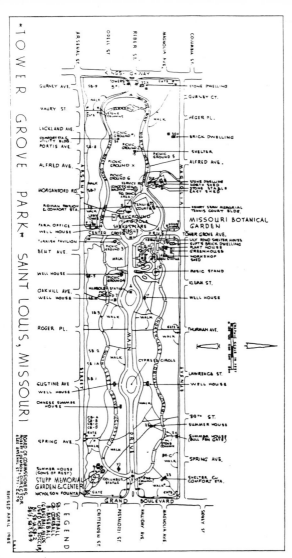

39 | THE MISSOURI BOTANICAL GARDEN

4344 Shaw, 63110; (314) 577-5100. Open 9am-8pm everyday, Memorial Day-Labor Day; 9am-5pm, rest of year. Small admission fee. Free for children under 13. Free W and S until noon. Trams and tours year round. Restaurant and gift shop.

Locally referred to as Shaw's Garden, this is the precious legacy of an English immigrant, Henry Shaw. His love for botany and the Kew Gardens of his native land brought the Botanical Garden to reality and the Garden, a 79-acre oasis of beauty in the midst of the city, opened its doors to the public in 1859. It is the oldest botanical garden in the United States and one of the most unique. Appreciating nature on a leisurely stroll along paths which wind through well-manicured lawns and flower beds, visitors view seasonal displays of flowers, English woodlands, a rose garden featuring 6,000 varieties of roses, an herb garden, water lily ponds, chimes, sculptures of famous artists, and fountains in an uncrowded natural setting. There is also a scented garden for the visually impaired. The 14-acre Japanese Garden, Seiwa-En, is the largest such garden on the North American continent with the most faithful replicas of natural waterfalls, beaches, and islands.

There are greenhouses:
- the Climatron, replete with waterfalls and the lush tropical foliage of rain forests;
- the Shoenberg Temperate House, displaying plants from regions with a Mediterranean climate;
- the Desert House, housing a collection of desert plants of the world.

The new Brookings Interpretive Center informs visitors on how they can help save the world's rain forests. The Garden is also an education and research center which collects, studies, and catalogs plants from all over the world. More than 125,000 adults and children benefit from the Garden's many education programs annually. The Kemper Center for Home Gardening, largest of its type in America, entertains and informs visitors of the joys of home gardening. The Japanese Festival is held every year in Aug and other functions are held throughout the year.

40 | THE HILL

Bordered by Hampton Ave, Kingshighway, I-44, and Fyler, the Hill, as St. Louis affectionately refers to it, is the home of a large Italian Community in the southwest part of the city. In the 1800s, the opening of clay mines attracted various ethnic groups to work in this area; this made St. Louis one of the most important brick and terra cotta centers in America. Over the years, the area became an Italian community. With the mines gone, the Hill has turned to the restaurant, pasta, lunchmeat, and construction industry, and gives St. Louis the best of Italy. Going to the Hill offers an escape from the pressures of life; it is like going home to a wonderfully prepared meal among people who know how to extend hospitality and their joy in living. There are many elegant and moderately priced indoor and outdoor Italian restaurants, entertainment, bocce alleys, groceries, and bakeries with specialties from Northern and Southern Italy. The Hill is also fondly remembered by St. Louisans as the home of baseball's Joe Garagiola and Yogi Berra.

41 ST. AMBROSE CHURCH
Wilson and Marconi Aves, 63110; (314) 771-1228.

St. Ambrose is a part of 12th century Italy in St. Louis, a jewel of Romanesque architecture. It is central to the lives of many of the Hill residents. The marbles, stained glass windows, and statues came from Italy. In front of the Church, Rudolph Torrini's sculpture, "The Italian Immigrants", is a reminder to future generations of their roots. The efforts displayed by the Italian-Americans on the Hill to maintain the stability and cohesiveness of their community has inspired other urban neighborhood renewals throughout the city.

South St. Louis County

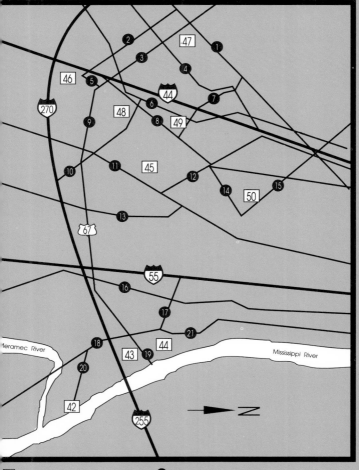

POINTS OF INTEREST
42 Golden Eagle River Museum
43 Jefferson Barracks Historical Park
44 Jefferson Barracks Cemetery
45 Grant's Farm
46 Laumeier Sculpture Park
47 The Magic House
48 The Thomas Sappington House
49 The Hawken House
50 The Oakland House

STREET
1 Manchester
2 Geyer
3 Kirkwood
4 Lockwood
5 Rott
6 Big Bend
7 Rock Hill Rd.
8 Watson Rd.
9 Lindbergh
10 Sappington

11 Gravois
12 Laclede Station Rd.
13 Tesson Ferry Rd.
14 Hegee Rd.
15 Genesta
16 Lemay Ferry Rd.
17 Reavis Barracks Rd.
18 Telegraph Rd.
19 Sheridan
20 Becker
21 Kingston

SOUTH COUNTY

42 GOLDEN EAGLE RIVER MUSEUM

Bee Tree Park, 63119; (314) 846-9073. River Museum and Nims Mansion: open May through Oct, W-S, 1-5pm. Free admission. Guided tours of the Mansion only, S and Su, 1-5pm; donation requested. Access: I-270 to Telegraph Rd, S., left on Becker, into Bee Tree Park, to the Nims Mansion.

The Golden Eagle Museum, located in the Nims Mansion in Bee Tree Park, was organized in 1942 by a group of ladies who had known the glorious days of the Golden Eagle Riverboat cruises on the Mississippi and were intent on preserving the memory of America's rivers and boats. The history of the life on the river is explained through a collection of models of riverboats of the 1800s, which includes flatboats, a Clermont, a cotton packet, sternwheelers, showboats, towboats, and other steamboats designed for particular purposes, such as "The Western Engineer", which was built for Major Stephen H. Long. James Monroe had commissioned Long to explore the Missouri River in 1819 and this curious serpent-looking steamboat was meant to terrify the Indians. All these were boats which plied the 16,000 navigable miles of the Mississippi River network and played a major role in America's development. A library of more than 500 books and photographs on life on the river is available by appointment. While at the Museum, visit the Nims Mansion and grounds high on the bluff overlooking the Mississippi. Though unfurnished, this 1927 mansion is a dream of a vacation home.

43 JEFFERSON BARRACKS HISTORIC PARK

533 Grant Rd, 63125; Visitor's Center: (314) 544-5714; Museum: 544-4154. Park and Museums open all year except Thanksgiving, Dec 25, and Jan 1. Museums and Visitor's Center open W-S, 10am-5pm; Su, Noon-5pm. Closed in Jan. Access: I-55, 255 east, North Telegraph Rd, North Kingston to Broadway and Grant.

Jefferson Barracks, established in 1826, stretched over 1,702 acres overlooking the Mississippi River, and was once the largest military post in America. Its strategic location helped open the West and protect American interests in the newly-acquired land. The post was appropriately named for Thomas Jefferson, whose Louisiana Purchase had made the expansion of the West possible. Across these grounds walked Zachary Taylor, Ulysses S. Grant, Robert E. Lee, General W.T. Sherman, Dr. W. Beaumont, Dwight Eisenhower, and many others whose names are familiar to Americans. In 1827, the Jefferson Barracks Cemetery was established on the post grounds. In 1946, Jefferson Barracks was deactivated, and 420 acres of land were given to the County and used as the Jefferson Barracks Historic Park; 135 acres became the home of the

Missouri Army and Air National Guard, and the remaining portion became known as the Jefferson Barracks National Cemetery. Jefferson Barracks' long and crowded history through the Civil War, the Spanish-American War, and World Wars I and II can be retraced with interest in the exhibits of the Jefferson Barracks Historic Park Museums: the Powder Magazine Museum, the CCC (Civilian Conservation Corps) Historic Museum, the old Ordnance Room, are available in this open-meadowed park which offers Laborers' House and Stable. Picnic facilities and corkball a scenic fields view of the Mississippi River. Special yearly events such as Hot Air Balloon Races and Indian Pow Wows are held in the Park.

44 JEFFERSON BARRACKS NATIONAL CEMETERY

Sheridan Rd, 63125; (314) 263-8691.
Office open M-F, 8am-4:30pm. Gates open daily, dawn to dusk.
Access: I-55, 255 east, North Telegraph Rd, turn right onto Sheridan.

Jefferson Barracks National Cemetery is the 4th largest cemetery in the nation. More than 100,000 veterans or their dependents, including Union and Confederate soldiers, are buried here. Maps of the cemetery are provided at the office for self-guided tours; a true walk through the past, among heroes who made today's freedom possible. Memorial Day veterans' events are held at the cemetery; moving ceremonies linking us to the past and recommitting us to strive for peace among men.

45 GRANT'S FARM

10501 Gravois, 63123; Tickets: (314) 843-1700. Admission and parking free. A train tour with some walking. Open mid-Apr through mid-Oct. Apr, May, Sept, and Oct, open Th-Su; Jun, Jul, and Aug, open T-Su; 6 tours daily at 9, 10, and 11am and at 1, 2, and 3pm. About 15 miles from downtown. Access from downtown: South on I-55, Lindergh exit, turn right onto Lindbergh, right onto Gravois, 2 miles on Gravois, turn left onto Grant Rd. Access from Airport: I-70W, I-270S, Gravois exit, turn left at Gravois, 3 miles on Gravois, turn left onto Grant Rd.

Grant's Farm, the home of the Anheuser-Busch family, is named after Ulysses S. Grant, who lived and farmed part of these grounds in 1856. A train, winding through the beautiful grounds of the Farm, takes the guest to Tier Garden, a small animal zoo where bird and elephant shows are held and children are allowed to bottle-feed baby goats; next, to Bauernhof, the Hospitality Terrace Cafe, where Busch beer is served, and stables, trophies, and the Busches' carriage collection can be seen. The train proceeds through game preserves where deer, antelope, buffalo, and zebras roam freely and where the impressive Rhine-like castle the Busches built in 1911 can be viewed. Also visible is the rustic cabin Grant built for himself and his St. Louis bride 12 years before his ascent from hard working but unsuccessful farmer to the Presidency. A fence made from 2,563 rifle barrels used during the Civil War faces Grant's cabin. The tour concludes with a visit to the world-famous Budweiser Clydesdale stables.

46 | LAUMEIER SCULPTURE PARK

Geyer and Rott Rds, 63127; (314) 821-1209. Open all year, 8am-sunset. Museum hours: T-S, 10am-5pm; Su, Noon-5pm; Jun through Aug, free Su evening concerts in the Park at 7pm. Free 1-hour guided tours on Su, May through Oct, at 2pm. Free cassettes also available for self-guided tours. Access: I-44 to Lindbergh Blvd, exit. South on Lindbergh, 1/2 mile to Rott Rd, right on Rott and 1/2 mile to park entrance. Wheelchair accessible.

Laumeier, one of the few major sculpture parks in the world, is a unique park for outdoor exhibition of contemporary art which has gained international recognition since it opened in 1976. Set on 96 scenic acres of rolling hills, the park is graced by over 60 modern sculptures which can be seen over a walk of 2 miles. A map, obtained at the Museum, indicates the location of the sculptures and names of the artists. Laumeier's outdoor sculpture collection reads like a "Who's Who" in contemporary art. Its collection contains one of the nation's leading concentration of site-specific sculptures—works by Vito Acconci, Jackie Ferrara, Richard Fleischner, Dan Graham, Jene Highstein, Mary Miss, Beverly Pepper, Ursula von Rydingsvard, and Robert Stackhouse. The expanse of the park provides the needed space these monumental and forceful sculptures require, and their selective placement adds a pleasant element of surpirse. Laumeier is a personal experience for both art and nature lovers. Exhibits in the Laumeier Museum change through the year, and a gift shop is available. Special events are held throughout the year; two of the largest ones: in May, The Contemporary Art and Crafts Fair, which attracts more than 150 artists from all parts of the U.S.; and in mid-Dec, Laumeier sponsors a spectacular 60-ton ice sculpture, "Fire and Ice", a display of ice, fire, lighting effects, and music, which draws thousands of visitors to the evening event.

47 | THE MAGIC HOUSE

516 S. Kirkwood Rd (S. Lindbergh), 63122; (314) 822-8900. Summer hours: T, Th, S, 10am-6pm; F, 10am-9pm; Su, Noon-6pm. During school year, open 1pm-5:30pm. Closed M. Small admission fee. First S of each month, 6-10pm, adults only. Third F of the month, family night, 6-9pm. Free admission

Children will ask to visit the Magic House again and again because it is a hands-on museum. The experience is educational, thrilling, and fun. There are more than 50 exhibits. Explore a human-size maze, touch an electrostatically charged ball, watch your hair stand on end, see your silhouette transformed into blotches of colors, observe amazing optical illusions and be ready for more surprises. There is even a section for children 1 to 7 years of age. Plan to spend at least 1½ hours.

48 THE THOMAS SAPPINGTON HOUSE

1015 S. Sappington Rd, 63126; (314) 957-4785; Tea-Room: 821-3223. Open all year for guided tours. Closed holidays. T-F, 11am-3pm; S, Noon-3pm. Small admission fee. A tea room serves lunch and cocktails. Gift shop. Access: I-44, Big Bend exit, east to Sappington Rd, south to Sappington House. From I-270, exit at Gravois Rd, east to Sappington, north to Sappington House. From I-55, exit at Lindbergh Blvd to Sappington Rd, then north approximately 4 miles to Sappington House.

The Thomas Sappington House, built in 1808 and exquisitely restored and furnished with period pieces, is one of the rarest examples of Federal architecture in St. Louis, and the oldest brick house in St. Louis County. The house, built by slaves with bricks made on site, once stood on 200 acres of land which Thomas had received from his father as a wedding gift. The house is a showcase of delicate antiques, and the Indian items on display throughout the house speak of friendly relations with the Indians of the area. The Library of Americana, the Tea Room in the Barn center, the house, and the old-fashioned flower and herb garden are an invitation to draw back and forget time for a while.

49 THE HAWKEN HOUSE

1155 S. Rock Hill Rd, 63119; (314) 968-1857.
Guided tours S-Su, 1-4pm, Mar to mid-Dec except Easter, Mother's Day, and Jul 4. Other tours by appointment. Call for information and schedules of interesting monthly exhibits and events. Admission fee. Access: I-44, exit Elm Ave, west on Big Bend to Rock Hill Rd, south.

This elegant Greek Revival farmhouse was built in 1857 by Christopher Hawken for his young bride, Mary Ann Eades. For a brief time, Christopher worked with his father Jacob and his uncle Samuel, famous gunsmiths based in the city of St. Louis. They made the Hawken rifles which played a vital part in the history of the West. The 2-story brick house, unlike many in the area, has closets and numerous large windows. The house is furnished with Victorian furniture dating from 1857 to the 1890s. In the parlor is a photograph of Ulysses S. Grant, a good friend and card-playing partner of Christopher's. There is also a replica of a Hawken rifle favored by Daniel Boone, John Fremont, Jim Bridger, and soldiers serving on the expanding frontier. On the basement level is a gift shop and a display of 600 dolls from around the world which were donated to the Webster Groves Historical Society to help promote better international understanding.

50 THE OAKLAND HOUSE

7801 Genesta, 63123; (314) 352-5654. Open only on the 3rd Su of the month from 1-4pm all year. Small admission fee. Access: I-44 to Laclede Station Rd exit; south to Heege Rd, turn left; 9 blocks to Genesta; turn left.

Oakland House was the country home of Louis Benoist, a prestigious French-Canadian banker in St. Louis and one of the richest men in the U.S. at that time. This palatial Italianate mansion was built by architect George Barnett in 1852 of white limestone quarried on the estate. Of special interest is a framed Letter of Nobility granted one of Benoist's ancestors, which is sealed by the King of France, Louis XIV; also, a beaded vest which Sitting Bull gave to Fr. DeSmet, a friend of the Benoists who came to the Oakland House to rest while in St. Louis.

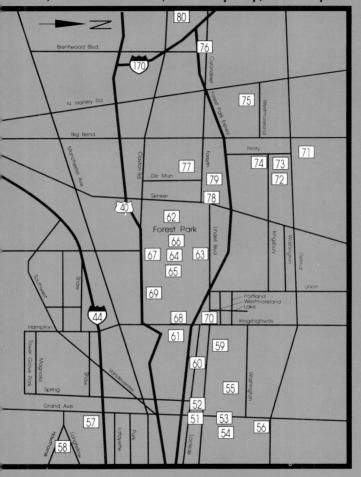

idtown, Central West End, University City, and Clayton

POINTS OF INTEREST

Midtown
51 St. Louis University
52 Cuppies House and
   McNamee Art Gallery
53 Vaughn Cultural Center-
   Urban League of
   Metropolitan St. Louis
54 Fabulous Fox Theatre
55 Sheldon Concert Hall
   and Ballroom
56 St. Louis Symphony
   Orchestra
57 Compton Hill Water Tower
58 Compton Heights

Central West End
59 Cathedral of Saint Louis
60 Bob Kramer's Marionettes
61 Barnes Hospital-W.U. Medical
   Center-Jewish Hospital and
   St. Louis Children's Hospital
62 Forest Park
63 History Museum (Missouri
   Historical Society)
64 Jewel Box
65 The Muny
66 St. Louis Art Museum
67 St. Louis Zoological Park
68 Steinberg Memorial Skating Rink
69 St. Louis Science Center
70 The Private Places

University City
71 University City's City Hall
72 Craft Alliance Gallery
73 St. Louis Conservatory and
   Schools for the Arts CASA
74 Center of Contemporary
   Arts-COCA

Clayton
75 Hanley House
76 St. Louis County
   Government Center
77 Concordia Historical Institute
78 Washington University
79 Washington University Art
   Gallery-Steinberg Hall
80 Ethical Society

MIDTOWN

51 ST. LOUIS UNIVERSITY
at the corner of Grand and Lindell Ave, 63103; (314) 658-2222.

A private, Catholic University in midtown, St. Louis University enrolls more then 11,000 local, national, and international students in more than 80 fields of study. Founded in 1818, this coeducational university, the oldest university west of the Mississippi, provides the St. Louis Community with 2 of every 5 attorneys and 1 of every 4 doctors in practice here. In 1909, it was the first university in North America to open a School of Geophysics. Today, the Department of Geophysics maintains and monitors the seismographic equipment of more than 45 stations in the central Mississippi Valley. St. Louis University has had a great influence upon St. Louis life and education and upon the urban renewal of the midtown area.

52 CUPPLES HOUSE AND McNAMEE ART GALLERY
3673 W. Pine Blvd, 63108; (314) 658-3025.
Small donation. Closed M and S. T-F, Noon-4pm; Su, 2-4pm.

This Chateauesque mansion, built by Samuel Cupples at the cost of a half a million dollars in 1890, is now owned by St. Louis University and is located on the campus. Samuel Cupples, a self-made man and a tycoon in wooden products, spared no expense on his home of 42 rooms with 22 fireplaces, lavish parquet floors and woodwork, and Tiffany stained glass of rare beauty. His generosity and civic mindedness contributed to the development of hospitals, orphanages, and schools. The basement of the house, once a bowling alley, is now a modern Art Gallery which houses the large and diverse art collection of St. Louis University and loan exhibits. The Gallery is a must for all art enthusiasts.

53 VAUGHN CULTURAL CENTER - URBAN LEAGUE OF METROPOLITAN ST. LOUIS
525 N. Grand, 63103; (314) 535-9227.
Open M-F, 10am-5pm. Free admission.

This art center features the work of local and national African-American artists. Programs include poetry reading, lectures, films, children's programs, and other special events.

54 THE FABULOUS FOX THEATRE
527 N. Grand, 63103; (314) 534-1678. Box office: 534-1111.
Tours available T, Th, S, 10:30am. Pick up ticket at 10am. Tours last about 1 hour.

Whether or not you see any performances at the Fox Theatre, you should at least tour this impressive theatre. The theatre was built in 1929 by C. Howard, an American movie palace architect who designed many other magnificent theatres in England and in the U.S. The Fox Theatre was a departure from his earlier designs of old world elegance. Designed after a Hindu Mosque, it cost about 1 and 1/2 million dollars to build. When grand theatres were in vogue, Wm. Fox, the owner of the Fabulous Fox, owned 805 other theatres throughout the country. The Fox was restored and reopened in 1982, and is now used to present the best of Broadway musicals and Las Vegas entertainment. In the summer, classic movies and, occasionally, organ concerts are presented on M nights. The Fox Wurlitzer organ, 1 of only 5 "Crawford Specials", was recently restored and the organ concerts are still one of the most unique attractions seen in St. Louis.

55 THE SHELDON CONCERT HALL AND BALLROOM
3648 Washington Ave, 63108; (314) 533-9900. Ample Parking.

The Sheldon, built as a memorial to the founder of the St. Louis Ethical Society, Walter L. Sheldon, was designed by Louis C. Spiering, principal architect of the 1904 World's Fair, for Chamber Music and lecturing. From its opening day in 1912, this elegant Greek Revival jewel has been recognized as having extraordinary acoustic qualities. When the Ethical Society moved to the county, The Sheldon was sold and used for various purposes until it was rediscovered, rescued, and restored from 1984 through 1986 to its original grandeur by Beverly Hills arts patron, Eugene Golden. This intimate 800+ seat gem was named one of the best-loved halls in America by touring musicians in 1990. Above the concert hall is a versatile and elegant Ballroom where kitchen, maple floors, skylights, beams, and stage create a unique and distinguished ambiance for a variety of social, artistic, and business functions for the entire community. It is today the busiest cultural center in St. Louis and its selective and varied programs are some of the most exclusive. For the fifth and final time in its colorful rich history, this treasure is changing hands. The Sheldon Arts Foundation has been established to acquire the landmark and guide its destiny as a not-for-profit public trust.

56 ST. LOUIS SYMPHONY ORCHESTRA
Powell Symphony Hall, 718 N. Grand Blvd, 63103; Box office: (314) 534-1700.

The St. Louis Symphony performs in Powell Hall, a beautiful building with excellent acoustics. The Symphony's programs feature world-renowned artists, including Jean Pierre Rampal, Yo-Yo Ma, Isaac Stern, Itzhak Perlman, and many others. It frequently offers free concerts throughout the city and under the Gateway Arch, and special concerts geared to young adults. A Pops Concert series featuring special guests and Richard Hayman, the famous harmonica-playing conductor, is held at Queeny Park (71), 533-2500 ext. 202.

57 COMPTON HILL WATER TOWER

Grand Ave and Russell.

Of America's original 400 water towers, only 7 remain; 3 of these are in St. Louis. The Compton Hill Water Tower rises to a height of 179 feet and dates to 1904, when the St. Louis Waterworks began distributing purified water. These water towers, now obsolete, are architectural and historic landmarks. Compton Hill has an observation deck which is open during special neighborhood events and is ideal for photography, offering a 360-degree view. In the summer there are free concerts in the park. Near the tower is a statue of a nude woman titled "Naked Truth"; it was given by the city's German community in 1914 to honor 3 German-American editors.

58 COMPTON HEIGHTS

Area located between I-44, Shenandoah, Nebraska, and Grand. To visit, enter from Grand Ave into Hawthorne or Longfellow.

Compton Heights private places were built in the late 1800s and early 1900s by many architects, including Julius Pitzman. Be sure to drive through these streets of majestic mansions. House tours are conducted occasionally and usually advertised in the Calendar section of the Post-Dispatch. Another source of information is the Visitors Bureau, (314) 242-1764.

CENTRAL WEST END

The Central West End, one of the most fashionable areas of St. Louis, reflects St. Louis' rich architectural history. Flanked by Forest Park, Washington University Medical Center, major hotels, major universities, and the sumptous mansions of the private places, the CWE is a neighborhood which attracts many professionals. Residents are within walking of the Maryland Ave shopping district and the cafes and smart boutiques of Euclid Ave. It is a place brimming with life, with ethnic restaurants, with entertainment, and more.

59 CATHEDRAL OF SAINT LOUIS
(New Cathedral)
Lindell Blvd and Newstead Ave; (314) 533-2824.
Open daily, 6am-6pm. Free tour every Su except Easter, 1pm.
Private tour arrangement for groups of 25-50 with small fee and 3 weeks notice required.

A glorious prayer of praise, magnificently written in stone; this is the Saint Louis Cathedral, which Pope Paul VI called "the outstanding Cathedral of the Americas". One of the show places of St. Louis, it is a "must" for the visitor. Built in 1907, this imposing edifice combines the best features of Byzantine and Romanesque architecture and boasts the largest collection of mosaics in the world. A huge green-tiled dome soars 227 feet above street level... higher than a 22-story building. While the exterior of the Cathedral is impressive, the interior is nothing less than awe-inspiring. The marble in the Cathedral comes from nearly every marble center in the world; over 70 different types are found in the sanctuary alone. Two rose windows are set in the north and south walls, but the most beautiful and descriptive work of art are the mosaics which light the domes, archways, and walls, telling the story of faith from creation to last judgment. Some 8,000 different shades of color and approximately 145,000,000 pieces of stone and glass have been incorporated in the mosaics which portray scenes from the Old and New Testaments, events in the Life of Saint Louis IX, King of France, and the men and women prominent in the history of the Catholic Church in North America and St. Louis. The installation of the mosaics was begun in 1912 and is now complete; the 84,000 square feet of mosaics which cover the walls of the Cathedral is the largest collection in the world. Centrally located in the Central West End, 3 blocks east of Forest Park, the Cathedral welcomes visitors. Plan a leisurely stay if you can. A full day might well seem less than adequate to exhaust the features of beauty and interest to be explored in one of St. Louis' most majestic landmarks.

60 BOB KRAMER'S MARIONETTES

4143 Laclede Ave, 63108; (314) 531-3313.
Open all year, T, W, Th, S. Fall, Winter, and Spring demonstrations at 1pm and shows at 2:15pm; Summer demonstrations at 10am and shows at 11:15am. Reservations required. Shows last 1½ hours. Puppet shows change seasonally. Gallery and gift shop open M-F, 10am-4pm.

The Bob Kramer's Marionettes Shows have delighted and inspired many an audience. The shows are cleverly divided into 2 parts, a studio demonstration followed by a puppet show. The demonstration introduces the audience to the history and art of puppetry, and to the different types of puppets. These demonstrations remove much of the secrecy cloaking puppetry and spark children's imagination. All performing puppets are made in the studio, and the productions are artistic and imaginative. A Gallery displays puppets from around the world and a gift shop has tempting and colorful selections of puppets. The puppets will also perform at birthday parties, fairs, festivals, and the like.

61 THE BARNES HOSPITAL - W.U. MEDICAL CENTER - JEWISH HOSPITAL - ST. LOUIS CHILDREN'S HOSPITAL

Kingshighway and Barnes Hospital Plaza, 63110.

Barnes Hospital, affiliated with the Washington University School of Medicine, has been operating for 75 years and is cited as one of the country's 5 best hospitals. It is a dynamic teaching hospital and healthcare center which has long attracted the brightest minds. The Medical Center is strengthened by the affiliations which exist between Barnes Hospital, the W.U. Medical School, Jewish Hospital, Children's Hospital, and the Central Institute for the deaf.

62 FOREST PARK

The park, surrounded by Kingshighway, Lindell, Skinker, and Highway 40, has 1,400 acres of rolling land. This was the location of the 1904 World's Fair held to commemorate the bicentennial of the Louisiana Purchase. The main attractions in the park are: The Jefferson Memorial; the Jewel Box; the Lagoon boat rides; the Saint Louis Art Museum; the Muny Opera; the Science Center; the golf courses; and the St. Louis Zoological Park.

orest Park

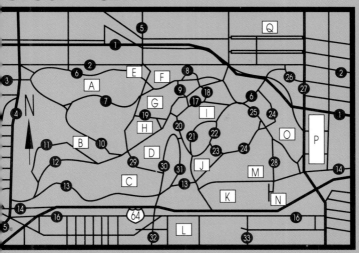

POINTS OF INTEREST	STREET	
A Golf Course	1 Forest Park Pkwy.	17 Theatre Dr.
B Art Museum	2 Lindell Blvd.	18 Deer Lake
C Zoo	3 Forsyth Blvd.	19 River Des Peres Dr.
D World's Fair Pavillion	4 Skinker	20 McKinley
E Jefferson Memorial	5 De Baliviere Ave.	21 Summit Dr.
F Lindell Pavillon	6 Grand Ave.	22 Union Dr.
G Davis Tennis Center	7 Lagoon Dr.	23 Macklind Dr.
H Boat Rides	8 Confederate Dr.	24 Wells Dr.
I Municipal Opera	9 Cricket Dr.	25 Jefferson Dr.
J Jewel Box	10 Fine Arts Dr.	26 West Pine Dr.
K Aviation Field	11 Valley Dr.	27 Kingshighway Blvd.
L Arena	12 Government Dr.	28 Faulkner Dr.
M Golf Course	13 Wells Dr.	29 Washington Dr.
N Science Center	14 Clayton Rd.	30 Concourse Dr.
O Steinberg Skating Rink	15 McCausland	31 Carr Lane Dr.
P Barnes Jewish	16 Oakland Ave.	32 Hampton
St. Louis Children's Hospital		33 Macklind Ave.
Q Central West End		

**(Courtesy of the St. Louis Department of Parks,
Recreation, and Forestry)**

63 THE HISTORY MUSEUM
(MISSOURI HISTORICAL SOCIETY)

Jefferson Memorial Building, Lindell and De Baliviere (in Forest Park), 63112; (314) 361-1424. T-Su, 9:30am-4:45pm. Free admission.

The Jefferson Memorial Building houses the History Museum operated by the Missouri Historical Society. It is the perfect place to begin visiting for a capsule look at St. Louis' past. It has 5 permanent galleries covering the history of St. Louis: Where Rivers Meet; Palaces in the Park: St. Louis and the 1904 World's Fair; The Lindbergh Gallery; The Volunteer Firefighting Gallery; and The Olin Gun Gallery. Other events and exhibits are offered through the year.

64 JEWEL BOX

in Forest Park, at the corner of McKinley and Wells Dr, 63110; (314) 531-0080. Open year round, 9am-5pm. Free admission M and T, 9am-Noon; other times, small admission fee.

The Jewel Box is a giant greenhouse which features seasonal flowers and plants. Many weddings are photographed in these surroundings. The outdoor garden has a Memorial to Korean War servicemen.

65 THE MUNY

in Forest Park, at McKinley and Theatre Dr, 63112; show information: (314) 361-1900; to charge tickets: 534-1111. Open daily, Jun through Aug. Admission fee. Free seats available 1 hour prior to each performance.

Since 1919, The Muny in Forest Park has committed itself to bringing Broadway's Best to one of the world's largest outdoor theatres. In addition, The Muny presents a Winter Broadway Series at the Fabulous Fox Theatre, Sept through May. Be sure to attend this traditional summer outing for a very pleasant evening under the stars...a delightful experience!

66 THE SAINT LOUIS ART MUSEUM

1 Fine Arts Dr, Forest Park, 63110; (314) 721-0067. Information: 721-0072. Open year round. Closed M; Open T, 1:30-8:30pm; W-Su, 10am-5pm. Closed Thanksgiving, Dec 25, and Jan 1. Free admission. Free conducted tours W through Su at 1:30pm. Fee for Special Exhibitions, but free to all on T.

The Palace of Fine Arts, built for the 1904 World's Fair, is an architectural masterpiece filled with masterpieces of art from all time periods and all cultures. There is something special at every turn, from ancient art, to Impressionism, to modern art. There are Period Rooms and a mummy with x-rays on display for a look inside. Then stop in the Museum Shop for everything from jewelry, posters, and cards, to "art treasures", and relax in the Museum

Cafe with views of Sculpture Terrace and Forest Park to provide the perfect setting for the perfect meal. Enjoy films, lectures, gallery talks, special performances, classes, and tours. It is always enjoyable to discover or rediscover this never-static Museum, one of the top 10 art museums in the nation!

67 THE ST. LOUIS ZOOLOGICAL PARK

in Forest Park, with entrances on Wells Dr, Washington Dr, Fine Arts Dr, and Government Dr, 63110; (314) 781-0900.
Lot parking is available. Open daily, 9am-5pm, except Dec 25 and Jan 1. Free admission. Wheelchairs available.

A must for everyone. The St. Louis Zoo, recognized as one of the best in the world, houses more than 3,400 animals living in natural habitats on 83 acres of Forest Park. The Zooline Railroad provides (at a small fee) a 1.5 mile, 20-minute narrated tour of the zoo with stops at 4 stations for exploring nearby exhibits. There is the Children's Zoo where children can get a close-up view of animals; the Aquatic House; lakes and islands filled with waterfowl; a walk-through bird cage which was built for the 1904 World's Fair; Big Cat Country; an Elephant House; the Jungle of the Apes with dense jungle foliage where only a 1½ inch thick glass panel separates the visitor from the apes. The Zoo has a Cheetah Survival Center to help propagate these endangered, graceful cats; Bear Pit exhibits; and The Living World, a unique education and discovery center that focuses on evolution, animal diversity, ecology, and conservation. A fascinating way to learn! Plan on spending a day at the Zoo!

68 STEINBERG MEMORIAL SKATING RINK

in Forest Park, Jefferson Dr, 63110; (314) 361-5103.
Roller skating mid-May through mid-Aug; Ice skating: mid-Nov through Mar (depending on weather). Call for times and fees. Private skating parties can be arranged. Free parking.

Steinberg Skating Rink is the 5th largest in the nation. It is a pleasure to ice skate in this beautiful park in the winter and roller skate to music in the summer; and if you do not know how, don't let that stop you: you can learn, at no extra cost. Large bonfires are lit every night in the winter next to the ice for, according to skaters' tradition, this means that it is "safe ice"; people gather around the fire to warm their hands, sing, drink hot cider, and join in fellowship.

69 ST. LOUIS SCIENCE CENTER

5100 Clayton Ave, in Forest Park, 63110; (314) 289-4400. Allow 1 hour minimum. Open M-Th, 9:30am-5pm; F-S, 9:30am-9pm; Su, 11am-5pm. Free admission to Exhibit Gallery, Monsanto Science Park, parking. Nominal fee for McDonnell Star Theater, Discovery Room, Science Showplace, and Sciencing Lab.

Located in the southeast corner of Forest Park, the St. Louis Science Center makes the world of science come alive and provides exciting challenges for all ages. Among the areas to visit are:

- Monsanto Science Park - life-size, playground-type outdoor exhibits that focus on weather, light, sound, motion, and energy.
- Exhibit Gallery - various hands-on displays on ecology, humanity, technology, and space sciences; experience an earthquake or launch a hot air balloon.
- Sciencing Lab - be a scientist-at-work with computers and various tabletop experiments.
- McDonnell Star Theater - 3 different planetarium shows (a main feature, children's show, and seasonal night sky presentation), enhanced by 3D DIGISTAR® computer graphics projector which produces spectacular special effects. The expanded science center facility, at nearby 5050 Oakland Ave, will open Nov. 1991.

70 THE PRIVATE PLACES

To see Westmoreland and Portland Places, enter Lake Ave from Lindell Blvd.

To see Kingsbury Place, Washington Terrace, and Waterman Place, enter west from Union Blvd.

Annual tours of these houses are sponsored by the Central West End Association, (314) 367-2220 for dates.

The Private Places originated in St. Louis. These enclaves, guarded by elegant gates and closed to public traffic, blossomed in west St. Louis in the 1880s while the town was experiencing an industrial boom. Entrepreneurs, politicians, and industrial barons built palatial houses with libraries, ballrooms, and the latest comforts and crazes of the times. These stately mansions, displaying a variety of architectural styles, astonished Royalty visiting the 1904 World's Fair. The homes remain showcases of elegance and reminders of the foresight that envisioned the World's Fair, that made St. Louis an industrial center, financed Charles Lindbergh's transatlantic flight, and initiated the Davis Cup in tennis—all factors which focused world attention on St. Louis and helped make it the city it is today.

UNIVERSITY CITY LOOP

Located 15 minutes from downtown, University City is a unique community. Founded in 1903 by E.G. Lewis, a colorful entrepreneur who dreamed of making his "University City" the home of his Woman's Magazine Publishing Company, and a national art center. His legacy continues, for University City is indeed a center of culture and learning. Although largely residential, the University Loop (so named because this is where streetcars used to turn around), 6200 through 6600 Delmar Blvd, is a fascinating area to visit. Close to Washington University, it is reminiscent of the Latin Quarter in Paris. This cosmopolitan area is a meeting place for students, artists, musicians, and literary people. There are sidewalk cafes, bookshops selling new and second-hand books in English and foreign language editions, night-clubs, exotic restaurants from Ethiopia, Lebanon, etc., cinemas which feature foreign films, bakeries, an open-air market, art galleries, and shops featuring arts from around the world. One can breakfast on croissants with classical music and visit 2 dynamic visual art centers: COCA and CASA.

It is a neighborhood where a short walk allows you to discover many entertaining facets. For a listing of the many creative monthly events, check the entertainment sections of the papers or call City Hall at (314) 862-6767; information concerning the Spring house tour is available at 726-0668.

Yearly, the city sponsors 7 exhibits by local artists at the University City Library.

71 UNIVERSITY CITY'S CITY HALL
6801 Delmar, 63130; (314) 862-6767.

University City's City Hall, an impressive 5-story octagonal tower structure built in 1903 by E.G. Lewis as the executive office building of his publishing company, is well-worth visiting. Rising to 135 feet, the building is a blend of many architectural styles. The windows are trimmed with terra cotta ornaments in the fashion of the day. The interior of the building is adorned by several murals depicting the activities of E.G. Lewis as a retailer, artist, idler, publisher, inventor, operator, builder, and businessman; a man of vision. Of special interest is the City Manager's office, once E.G. Lewis'. The University City Loop exit, at the corner of Trinity and Delmar, is guarded by George Julian Zolnay's Lion Gates, the symbol of University City. Guided tours are available by calling the City Hall.

72 CRAFT ALLIANCE GALLERY

6640 Delmar, 63130; (314) 725-1151. T-F, Noon-5pm; S, 10am-5pm. Free admission.

The gallery holds 6 to 8 exhibits by national artists each year. These feature contemporary works made from materials such as textiles, ceramics, wood, clay, glass, and metal. The gallery also has an education center for children and adults, and a gift shop featuring original, functional gifts.

73 THE ST. LOUIS CONSERVATORY AND SCHOOLS FOR THE ARTS - CASA

560 Trinity Ave at Delmar, 63130; (314) 863-3033, 10am-4pm for information or tickets.

CASA, a Conservatory and Schools for the Arts, offers recitals and concerts such as the Mae Whitaker Great Artists Series which feature performers who represent the highest achievements in this profession. An evening at CASA is never forgotten...Of special interest are the unique Japanese Suzuki methods the Conservatory uses to teach young children to play violin, cello, and guitar, and the Mae M. Whitaker International Competition (open for public attendance), encourages young artists to pursue concert careers.

74 THE CENTER OF CONTEMPORARY ARTS - COCA

524 Trinity Ave, 63130; (314) 725-6555 for information or tickets.

The Center of Contemporary Arts is a visual and performing arts center. Its modern and airy building, designed by renowned architect Eric Mendelsohn and listed in the National Register of Historic Places, was once a Synagogue. Renovated in 1986, it is now the perfect home to more than 30 art organizations and artists who lease rehearsal and performance space. This exciting and versatile center features a variety of musicians and dance and theatre groups, many world-renowned. The Gallery features internationally recognized exhibits year round. Also of interest are the special dance, music, and theatre educational programs, the children's creative theatre series, and the select international foreign film series presented weekly. Call the center for times and information.

CLAYTON

Centrally located, Clayton is a community of 2½ square miles with a significant central business district (10%) where over 30,000 business people work each day. Clayton has a small community atmosphere with big city amenities. There is a diversity of office spaces, new developments, and quality hotels with abundant support services nearby. Clayton boasts quality specialty retail and a diversity of restaurants. Highly sought-after residential property, a premier school district, and outstanding municipal services make for a superb quality of life in a well-planned community of 14,000 residents.

75 THE HANLEY HOUSE
7600 Westmoreland, 63105; (314) 727-8100, ext. 290
Open to the public, F-Su, 1-5pm. Guided tours available by appointment W, Th, and F mornings, 9:30am-Noon. Closed holidays. Small admission fee.

The Hanleys, originally from Virginia, built this typical Southern plantation farmhouse in 1855 and settled in Clayton. Standing today on the only acre left of hundreds, this 2-story house with its magnificent portico is the oldest in Clayton and one of the few restored farms in this country located in the midst of a prosperous community. It is guarded by a black oak tree estimated by the Missouri Department of Conservation to be 300 years of age, the oldest of its kind in Missouri. The House is furnished with 1860-1890 period furniture. Heated arguments revolved around restoring the "outhouse", but all decided in favor of it. Fall festival: 3rd week-end of Sept.

76 ST. LOUIS COUNTY GOVERNMENT CENTER
7900 Carondelet, 63105; (314) 889-2000.

Completed in the 1970s, the St. Louis County Government Center replaced the Old Courthouse which had been built in the 1870s, renovated in the 1950s, and which still occupied the site donated by Clayton and Hanley for the first Clayton Courthouse. Once established, the Clayton Courthouse became the seat of County Government and remained so as the County steadily increased in population.

77 CONCORDIA HISTORICAL INSTITUTE
801 DeMun Ave, 63105; (314) 721-5034, ext. 320. Open all year, 8:30am-4:30pm except S and Su. Appointment required for Seminary tour; call 721-5934, ext. 348.

The vast campus of the Concordia Seminary is so well hidden that no one would ever suspect its presence. The Concordia Historical Institute, located on the campus of Concordia Seminary, has won the reputation of being the "Smithsonian of Lutheranism" in the U.S. The Institute's Library owns an incredible collection of books, manuscripts, documents, letters, photogrpahs, biographical records, and historical artifacts, and is the ideal place for American Lutherans to trace their genealogy. Permanent exhibitions show interesting aspects of early Lutheran life in Europe and America. A log cabin built in 1938, a replica of the first building of Concordia Seminary in Perry County, can also be seen on the Concordia Seminary grounds.

78 WASHINGTON UNIVERSITY
Skinker and Lindell Blvds, 63130; (314) 889-5000.

Washington University, a non-profit private school, was founded in 1853 by Wm. Greenleaf Eliot (the grandfather of T.S. Eliot, the St. Louis Poet). Its imposing Towers, copied after Windsor Castle, overlook the community at large and are a reminder of the vital role the University has in the cultural life of St. Louis. During the World's Fair, the University was exhibited as a model campus, hosted the first Olympics in America, and received the many guests to the Fair. The University has earned international recognition for the excellence of its teaching and research and offers more than 80 programs and 1,600 courses leading to degrees in Arts and Science, Architecture, Medicine, Engineering, Law, Social Work, Business Administration, and more. W.U. Medical School, affiliated to the Barnes Hospital Medical Center, is regarded as one of the best in the country. This intellectually stimulating center of learning and research has been honored with 16 Nobel Laureates.

79 WASHINGTON UNIVERSITY GALLERY OF ART - STEINBERG HALL
Skinker and Lindell Blvds, 63130; (314) 889-5490, or 889-4523. M-F, 10am-5pm; S and Su, 1-5pm. Closed holidays. Free admission. Wheelchair accessible.

Steinberg Hall, located on the Washington University Campus, exhibits the University's permanent collection of paintings and sculptures and special loan exhibits. Faculty shows are given every Fall and lectures are held regularly. Call for informaiton.

80 ETHICAL SOCIETY
9001 Clayton Rd, 63117; (314) 991-0955. Su, 9am - 1pm; M-F, 9am - 3pm.

The Ethical Society of St. Louis is the 4th oldest and the largest Ethical Society in the U.S. It relocated near Clayton in 1963 in an interesting building of Far Eastern architecture. The Society, dedicated to the supreme aim of creating a more humane society, offers many programs and workshops, and welcomes everyone, especially to the 11am Su Platform lectures given from the 3rd Su in Sept through the end of May. There are also art shows which feature local artists during business hours and on Su from 9am-3pm in the Ethical Society Hall. The Society also co-sponsors the University of Missouri-St. Louis Premiere Musical Performances.

West County

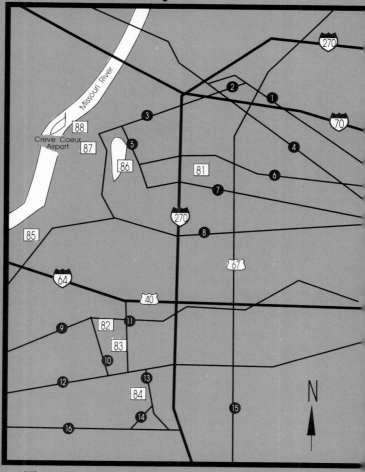

POINTS OF INTEREST
81 West Port Plaza
82 Queeny Park
83 Dog Museum
84 National Museum
   of Transport
85 Faust Park-St. Louis
   Carousel-Thornhill
86 Creve Coeur Lake
87 St. Louis Aviation
   Museum
88 Historic Aircraft
   Restoration Museum

STREET
1 Natural Bridge
2 McKelvey
3 Creve Coeur Mill
4 St. Charles Rock Rd.
5 Marine
6 Dorsett
7 Page
8 Olive St. Rd.

9 Clayton Rd.
10 Weidmann
11 Mason Rd.
12 Manchester
13 Barrett Station
14 Dougherty Ferry Rd.
15 Lindbergh Blvd.
16 Big Bend

WEST COUNTY

81 WEST PORT PLAZA
I-270 at Page, 63146; (314) 878-0400. About 25 miles from downtown.

West Port Plaza...Your passport to excitement. Where should visitors in the St. Louis area go to sample international cuisines, see great performances, and browse through boutiques and specialty shops, without crossing the street? West Port Plaza! The world of West Port Plaza offers visitors a unique blend of international charm and modern American convenience. The Plaza's two luxury hotels, 29 gift, fashion, and specialty shops, theatres, and international restaurants make it an ideal destination for excitement. It is a passport to the old and the new, the exotic and the familiar, the national and the international; and it's all waiting at the wonderful world of West Port Plaza.

82 QUEENY PARK
550 Weidman Rd, Ballwin, MO, 63011; (314) 391-0900.

Queeny Park can be entered from Mason Rd or Weidman Rd, but no roads within the Park connect these two entrances. Queeny Park's 569 acres of gentle rolling hills offer several recreational facilities:
- From the Weidman Rd entrance, an outdoor swimming pool, an indoor and outdoor skating rink, tennis courts, and the Greensfelder Recreation Complex which offers exhibits and various events, including the St. Louis Symphony Summer Queeny Pops series. For event information, 534-1700. Special event: A National Horse Show is held in the 3rd week of Sept.
- From the Mason Rd entrance, the Park has horse trails, biking trails, picnic facilities, and The Dog Museum. Hayrides in the fall.

83 THE DOG MUSEUM
1721 S. Mason Rd in Queeny Park, 63131; (314) 821-DOGS.
Open M-S, 9am-5pm; Su, 1-4pm all year except Memorial Day, Thanksgiving, Dec 24, 25, 31, Jan 1, and Easter. Small admission fee.

The Dog Museum, a fine art museum long cherished by New Yorkers, moved to St. Louis in 1987, and has since added a new wing of 14,000 square feet. Its impressive collection of paintings and bronze sculptures and informative exhibits housed in the Jarville House and the new wing, depict the many breeds of dogs, the service and companionship dogs offer, and an introduction to the dog in art. The galleries cover six subjects: Show Dogs; Working Dogs; Hunting Dogs; The Dog as a Pet; Famous Dogs; and the Hall of Fame of dogs that have gained fame in movies, literature, or because of their heroic actions. The Museum has rotating exhibits, educational programs, and an interesting research library. The historic Jarville House, built in 1853, is an outstanding example of Greek Revival architecture in St. Louis County. Special event: Dog Days on the 3rd week-end of Sept.

84 NATIONAL MUSEUM OF TRANSPORT

3015 Barrett Station Rd, 63122-3398; (314) 965-7998. Open daily, 9am-5pm. Closed Thanksgiving, Dec 25, and Jan 1. Guided tours 9:30am-3:30pm. Admission fee. Free parking. Group rates. Access: From the north: 270, Big Bend exit, right onto Barrett Station Rd. From the south: 270, Dougherty Ferry Rd exit, left onto Barrett Station Rd.

The National Museum of Transport, begun in 1944 with the acquisition of Bellefontaine, an 1880 mule-drawn St. Louis street-car, is a repository of the last 150 years of transport. The 70-acre Museum, located by Barrett tunnel, one of the first 2 railroad tunnels built by the Pacific Railroad west of the Mississippi, is owned by St. Louis County Parks and Recreation. It has one of the most extensive railroad collections in the U.S. Also included are vintage buses, automobiles, streetcars, a towboat, and aircraft which reflect the importance transport played in the development of the U.S. and its ever-changing aspects. The Museum is a Memory Lane to many, where the beauty and struggles of the past can be relived, and an education to those who never knew this golden era. Also to be seen are: the oldest stagecoach in existence; the Truman and Vanderbilt private cars; a Frisco mail car; a milk tank car; "Big Boy", the world's largest modern steam locomotive; "Centennial", the largest diesel electric locomotive ever built; and many more interesting displays. Plan a stay of 2 to 3 hours...and that may not be enough time. Special events: Car Shows in the Spring and Summer.

85 FAUST COUNTY PARK — ST. LOUIS CAROUSEL — THORNHILL

15185 Olive Blvd, 63107; (314) 537-0222, or 889-3356.
This park offers 3 facilities: the St. Louis Carousel; the Thornhill Historic Site; and the Faust Historic Village, which is not currently open to the public.
The Carousel is open Feb-Dec 31, W-Su, Noon-5pm. Small fee. Thornhill is open W-Su, Noon-5pm. Small fee. Tours on the hour (532-7298).

Children will be thrilled to ride The St. Louis Carousel at Faust Park. This Carousel of more than 60 hand-carved animals, made in 1920 by the Dentzel Co of Philadelphia, was used for over 30 years at Forest Park Highlands until the amusement park was destroyed by fire. Rescued and restored to its original beauty, it has conveniently been installed in the Carousel Building, which allows it to operate regardless of weather. The Carousel Building also houses a gallery which displays changing exhibits of Folk Art: toys, tapestries, etc.

Thornhill, built c. 1817 by Frederick Bates, the second Governor of Missouri, is the oldest Governor's residence in existence in the state. Its location on the scenic and breezy Missouri Bluffs was probably chosen for its easy access by ferry to St. Charles, then the Capital of Missouri. The House's high ceilings and fine woodwork reflect the style of Governor Bates' native Virginia. His appointment in 1807 as Secretary of the New Louisiana Territory brought him to St. Louis and in 1824, he became Governor of Missouri but died the following year. His simple grave in the family plot near his home speaks loudly to family ties stronger than his need for public recognition and remembrance. Archeological investigations of the Missouri Bluffs near Thornhill indicate the presence of Indian settlements at a very early date. The Faust Folk Festival is held yearly on the 1st week-end of Oct. For other special events and festivals, call 532-7298. Every 3rd Su of the month, Apr through Sept, a craft festival is held at the House and free tours are offered on that day.

86 CREVE COEUR LAKE
Dorsett Rd and Marine Ave, Maryland Heights, MO, 63043.

Only 18 miles from downtown, Creve Coeur Lake, located in Creve Coeur Park, is a beautiful 320-acre lake, ideal for picnics, fishing, sailing, and water skiing. The lake acquired its puzzling name of "Heart-Breaker" from the French who settled in the area in the 1700s. Many legends have surrounded this name, though none has clearly authenticated the French "Heart-Breaker" and the belle involved. In 1933 and 1957, remains of Hopewell Indians dating to 120 B.C. were found on the grounds. Festival: Classic Drag Boat Races, a national competition during the 2nd week of Jun. Water ski competition in mid-Aug. For information regarding other events, call (314) 889-2222

87 ST. LOUIS AVIATION MUSEUM
3127 Creve Coeur Mill Rd, Maryland Heights, MO, 63043; (314) 524-1599. Open S and Su, 10am-4pm, May through Oct.

The St. Louis Aviation Museum was established in 1982 to preserve the substantial contributions St. Louis made to the development of aviation, contributions which make it one of the most significant aviation centers in the world. The Museum collection includes more than 13 vintage aircraft, a Phantom, a Banshee, a Voodoo, a Harrier, 5 engines, a WWII simulator, gas and hot air balloons, parachutes, instrument collection, aviation paintings, photographs, memorabilia, and more. Of interest also are an Apollo space suit, and "The City of St. Louis" basket of the 35,000 cubic-foot helium balloon Nikki Caplan and Jane Buckles sailed in 1982 to set a new world's distance record. The Museum is quick to point out the many "firsts" of St. Louis Aviation History. To cite a few: the first commercial airliner (Benoist Flying Boat) was produced in St. Louis in 1913; the first aviation school in the U.S. was Parks College of St. Louis, established in 1927; the first parachute jump from an airplane took place at Jefferson Barracks in 1912; America's first astronauts orbited the Earth in St. Louis-made Mercury and Gemini spacecraft; the list is incredibly long. Plans to move the Museum to an 11-acre facility at the Spirit of St. Louis Airport in Chesterfield are now in progress. Yearly, Vintage Aircraft Days Festivals are held at the end of May and end of Sept. For information regarding monthly events, call 524-1559.

88 HISTORIC AIRCRAFT RESTORATION MUSEUM
3127 Creve Coeur Mill Rd, St. Louis, MO, 63146; (314) 434-3368. Open S and Su, 10am-4pm and by appointment M-F.

The Creve Coeur Historic Aircraft Restoration Museum contains a collection of 75 classic and antique aircraft more than 40 years old, many from the '20s and '30s, including Monocoupes and Curtisses which were manufactured in St. Louis, Timms, Stinsons, Wacos, Ryans, Rawdons, and many more...This museum is unique in that these individually owned planes are not just displayed memories of the past, but planes restored and flown. Many are used to train pilots and provide unsurpassed experiences. The restoration facilities and advising team, the pilot training program, and the availability of both asphalt and grass landing strips draw people from all over. The atmosphere of this airport, not to mention the spirit and enthusiasm, is a living tribute to the early St. Louis Aviation pioneers. One of the special yearly events at the airport is The Annual Classic Aeroplane Rendez-vous held in Jul. More than 30 of these planes have participated in the Annual National Oshkosh Competition held in Wisconsin in Aug and have repeatedly won awards.

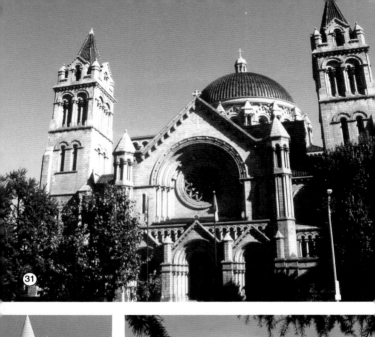

North County

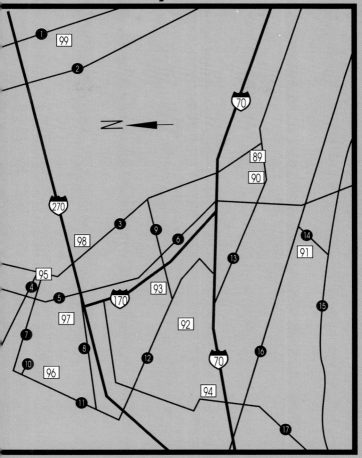

POINTS OF INTEREST
89 The Wilson Price Hunt House
90 The University of Missouri-St. Louis
91 Bearden Violin Shop
92 Lambert-St. Louis International Airport
93 McDonnell Douglas Prologue Room
94 Payne-Gentry House
95 Florissant Valley Chamber of Commerce
96 Museum of Western Jesuit Missions
97 Myers House
98 Taille de Noyer House
99 General Daniel Bissell House

STREET
1 Bellefontaine Rd.
2 Lewis & Clark Blvd.
3 New Florissant Rd.
4 St. Catherine
5 Graham Rd.
6 N. Hanley Rd.
7 Charbonnier
8 Dunn Rd.

9 Airport Rd.
10 Keevan
11 Howdershell Rd.
12 James S. McDonnell Blvd.
13 Natural Bridge Rd.
14 Lackland
15 Midland
16 St. Charles Rock Rd.
17 Fee Fee Rd.

NORTH COUNTY

89 THE WILSON PRICE HUNT HOUSE

7717 Natural Bridge Rd, 63121; Tours by appointment: (314) 383-7937; Garrett Gallery: 381-3022. Open T-F, Noon-4pm; S, 9:30am-3pm; Gallery reception 1st Su of month 1-4pm. Closed Thanksgiving, Dec 25, and Jan 1. Free Admission.

The Hunt House, built in the 1800s by Wilson Price Hunt, is the only residence remaining of the Lucas and Hunt families who helped develop St. Louis and the Normandy area of St. Louis County. This elegant house, a symbol of the area's heritage, exemplifies the new expression of architecture Americans were developing at that time. The Garrett Gallery, located in the Wilson Price Hunt House, a cooperative of 40 local artists, holds a most interesting national exhibition during the second week of Apr. Special events held 4 times a year, quilt shows, handicrafts; call for information.

90 UNIVERSITY OF MISSOURI - ST. LOUIS

8001 Natural Bridge Rd, 63121; (314) 553-5451.

While the University of Missouri heritage dates back to 1839, the young University of Missouri-St. Louis campus is quickly gaining its own rich history. From its beginning 27 years ago on a former country club grounds, the University of Missouri-St. Louis has grown to a large modern campus of some 22 buildings on 178 acres, offering complete services for all activities of a full university experience. The University's curriculum now includes 38 undergraduate programs, 22 masters programs, 7 professional programs, 6 doctoral programs, and 1 professional degree program. There are opportunities and programs as diverse as the student population's needs. Now the 3rd largest university in the state, UM-St. Louis, with a student body of nearly 13,000, is the major supplier of college-educated citizens to the St. Louis region. The University annually enrolls traditional college students (18 to 22-year-olds), but also, in increasing numbers, mature adults; UM-St. Louis also has more minority students than any other public university in Missouri. A vibrant, public, urban University with a qualified and motivated faculty and staff, the University of Missouri-St. Louis is determined to continue its recent history of growth and excellence.

91 THE BEARDEN VIOLIN SHOP

8787 Lackland, 63114; (314) 427-7570.
Tours are available by appointment. Free admission.

If you've wondered how violins were made and never had the opportunity to see how, this is your chance! The Bearden Violin Shop, now in its 3rd generation, is the oldest violin shop in St. Louis. It has played a significant role in making St. Louis a city of music by supplying finely crafted violins to professional musicians and providing exposure to this art. The shop's craftsmen, all seasoned violinmakers and graduates of violinmaking schools, offer seminars and demonstrations of all aspects of violin construction, making this intricate art seem simple. To cite but a few facts, it takes 200 hours, over 70 parts, and 132 meticulous steps to assemble a violin. The owner, a member of the prestigious International Society of Violin and Bow Makers, fondly recalls how an accident to a family violin led P.C. Bearden, his father, an expert cabinet maker, into the art of restoring and then creating The "Bearden Violin". Gentle classical music in the background and the displayed violins give the shop an aura of elegance. The photo gallery of international artists and the autographs acknowledging and thanking their "World's Best Shop", attest to the world-wide recognition this shop has gained.

92 | LAMBERT-ST. LOUIS INTERNATIONAL AIRPORT
10701 Natural Bridge Rd, 63145; (314) 426-8000.

Lambert-St. Louis International Airport is the 7th busiest commercial airport in the nation and the 13th busiest in the world. In spite of the airport traffic, passengers can easily get in and out of the airport and reach any point in the city within an half-hour. The airport is surrounded by well-developed neighborhoods which include hotels, shopping centers, restaurants, and entertainment for travelers. Once the stomping ground of Charles Lindbergh, the dare-devil pilot who won the hearts and backing of St. Louisans, the airport is named for Albert Bond Lambert, one of Lindbergh's original supporters and one of the most influential men in the airport's development. The thin-shelled concrete structure of Lambert Airport, designed by Minoru Yamasaki, and constructed in 1956, became a terminal trend-setter. The spacious and bright interior conveys a spirit of loftiness. A replica of Charles Lindbergh's "Spirit of St. Louis" and his original monocoupe are displayed in the main terminal. On the lower level, 2 magnificent murals, one painted by Siegfried Reinhardt, the other by Spencer Taylor, pay tribute to men and women in American Aviation.

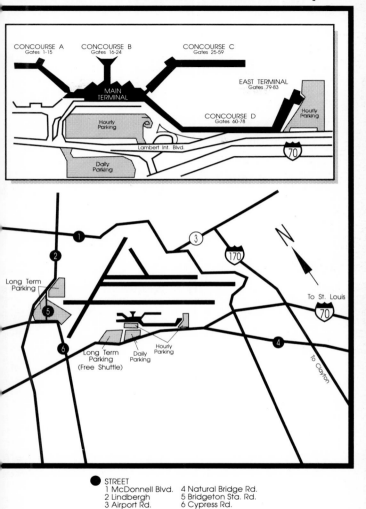

STREET
1 McDonnell Blvd. 4 Natural Bridge Rd.
2 Lindbergh   5 Bridgeton Sta. Rd.
3 Airport Rd.   6 Cypress Rd.

(Courtesy of Lambert-St. Louis International Airport)

93 THE McDONNELL DOUGLAS PROLOGUE ROOM

McDonnell Blvd and Airport Rd, 63166; (314) 232-5421.
Open Jun-Aug (T after Memorial Day until F before Labor Day),
T-S, 9am-4pm; Admission and parking free.

Aviation enthusiasts will want to visit the Prologue Room, located in the McDonnell Douglas Headquarters Building (the dark-colored building). The Prologue Room displays models and exhibits of aircraft, rockets, and aerospace technology developed in St. Louis since the company opened in 1939. A replica of a Mercury capsule that took the first man into space is on display.

94 THE PAYNE-GENTRY HOUSE

4211 Fee Fee Rd, Bridgeton, MO, 63044; (314) 739-5599.
Open S, 1-4pm. Closed during Jan.

The Payne-Gentry House, a Victorian structure built in 1870, was the summer home of Mary Elizabeth and Elbridge Gerry Payne. The charmingly restored house, with original furnishings, provides a look into a doctor's office of the late 1800s, a time when the doctor was doctor, surgeon, and dentist, all at the same time, and still found the time and energy to go to his patients' homes. Dr. William Payne's amputating set and other surgical instruments are on display.

95 THE FLORISSANT VALLEY CHAMBER OF COMMERCE

1060 St. Catherine, Florissant, MO, 63031; (314) 831-3500. A drive of 20 miles from downtown, or 2 miles from the airport. Access: I-270 to Florissant Rd. Self-guided tour outlines available.

Florissant, a French name meaning the "Valley of Flowers", was founded in 1786 by French settlers. The Florissant Valley Chamber of Commerce offers maps for self-guided tours of Florissant's historic homes. Maps can be obtained by calling the Chamber of Commerce at the number above, or by visiting the office. The annual Valley of Flowers Festival is held on the first week-end in May. For information regarding conducted tours of Florissant's historic homes, call Historic Florissant at 837-3903.

96 THE MUSEUM OF WESTERN JESUIT MISSIONS

700 Howdershell Rd, Florissant, MO, 63031; For tour information, (314) 361-5122 on weekdays or 837-3525 on Su. Open T and Th, 10am-3pm; Su, 1pm-4pm, Mar-Dec. Donation.

The Museum of Western Jesuit Missions at old St. Stanislaus on Seminary Ridge brings to life the significant role the Jesuits played in the westward expansion as missionaries, explorers, and educators. First established in 1823, a log cabin served as both a seminary and a school for Indians. The school, a first in American history, had the support of Bishop DuBourg and President Monroe. The Greek Revival building which houses the museum was built in 1840 by the seminarians who fired the bricks, used the limestone from nearby quarries, and made woodwork from their walnut trees. The museum has records, tools, and displays of the work of early pioneer priests, of DeSmet's labors with the Indians of the West, the only Metz organ left in the area, a collection of unsigned Madonna oil paintings, gold chalices and monstrances of intricate European art, and ancient global maps of the New World. A most interesting place to visit...

97 | THE MYERS HOUSE AND BARN

180 W. Dunn Rd, Florissant, MO, 63031; (314) 837-7661. Hours for House: M-S, 10am-4pm except T, W, 10am-8pm. Closed Su and Holidays. Hours of the Barn: M-S, 10am-4pm. Closed Su and Holidays. Access: I-270, Graham-Hanley exit, west on Dunn Rd.

Built in 1869, the Myers House, a Victorian structure with tiered porches gently overlooking the hurried pace of our 20th century highways, is now occupied by a deli-restaurant and unique antique and craft shops. It has an exceptional weaving and quilting center and one of the largest selections of cotton, silkened cotton, and blocks in the city. It is a delightful place to have lunch and spend an afternoon.

98 | THE TAILLE DE NOYER HOUSE

1896 S. Florissant Rd, Florissant, MO, 63032; (314) 524-1100. Open S and Su, 1-5pm, all year. Small admission fee.
Access: I-270, exit New Florissant Rd, south to first stop sign, right onto McCluer High School grounds, first right into Rue Taille de Noyer.

Taille de Noyer, so named because of its location in a walnut grove, was originally used as an Indian trading post. Built in 1790, it is one of the oldest houses in Florissant, and a good example of French architecture of that time. This inviting house has interesting and massive furnishings of the period. Of interest is a dog-trot, a blanket roller, a mattress smoother, a very unusual art piece made of plaited hair, a porcelain two-faced doll, and much more...

99 | THE GENERAL DANIEL BISSELL HOUSE

10225 Bellefontaine Rd, 63137; (314) 889-3356.
Open S and Su, Noon-5pm. Open all year, except Jan. Access: I-270 to Bellefontaine exit, south on Bellefontaine, 1 mile to Bissell House.

The General Daniel Bissell House, an imposing example of Federal architecture from 1812, was the home of Daniel Bissell, whose appointment as Commander of Upper Louisiana Territory brought him to St. Louis. He was named General in 1815 and remained in command of Fort Bellefontaine, a military post near the Mississippi-Missouri confluence, until Jefferson Barracks replaced the post in 1826. He chose to retire in St. Louis to this home he fondly called "Franklinville Farm". This spacious home contains many of the original furnishings, interesting items, military uniforms, and the various army commissions the general received signed by Presidents Washington, Madison, and Jefferson. Of interest is a collection of the curious and whimsical sculptures of John Rogers, then very popular, which depict aspects of life at the time. The Bissell Country Craft Fair is held at the house on the first week-end of Jun.

North St. Louis

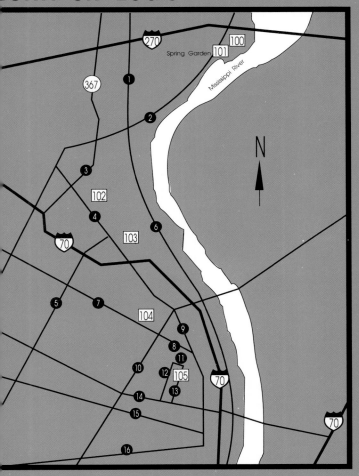

POINTS OF INTEREST
100 North Riverfront Park
101 Chain of Rocks Train Ride
102 Calvary Cemetery
103 Bellefontaine Cemetery
104 Fairgrounds Park
105 Black Repertory Company

STREET
1 Bellefontaine Rd.
2 Riverview Dr.
3 Riverview Blvd.
4 West Florissant Rd.

5 Kingshighway
6 Broadway
7 Natural Bridge Rd.
8 Palm St.
9 North Florissant Rd.
10 Grand Blvd.
11 St. Louis Ave.
12 Parnell
13 23rd St.
14 Cass Ave.
15 Delmar
16 Lindell Blvd.

NORTH ST. LOUIS

North St. Louis is the city's oldest neighborhood. It was the site of one of the original fields where settlers worked to provide staples for the St. Louis village. There were about a dozen mounds along the northern part of the riverfront, north of Biddle St, and records report the largest mounds at the northeast corner of Broadway and Mound St, which gave the city its nickname of "Mound City". Most of these have given way to urban development. It was only in 1869 that evidence indicated that these were Indian burial grounds. Primarily German, Irish, and Jewish immigrants settled in North St. Louis.

100 NORTH RIVERFRONT PARK
Riverview Dr at Spring Garden. Access: I-270, exit Riverview Dr, south on Riverview Dr for 1½ miles.

This park beautifully borders the Mississippi River for miles and provides for a lazy summer evening of fishing or picnicking along the river in the old-fashioned St. Louis style. Not many trees, an open park. Photograph enthusiasts can go up the hill from any Riverview Dr entrance and steal breathtaking views of the Gateway arch skyline. In the middle of the Mississippi River, two Intake Water Towers of interesting architecture can be seen. These towers, built in the late 1800s and now listed as National Landmarks, were occupied by ice-watchers whose work in the winter was to prevent ice from blocking water plant intake lines. They and their families lived in these houses which riverboat navigators used as landmarks.

101 CHAIN OF ROCKS TRAIN RIDES
Railroad Station at the entrance of North Riverfront Park at Riverview Dr and Spring Garden; (314) 752-3148.
Apr-Oct, 2nd Su of the month, 1-5pm. Special seasonal theme rides. Small admission fee.
Access: I-270, Riverview exit, south on Riverview Dr to North Riverfront Park.

Supported by the American Association of Railroaders, this full-size train has a diesel engine, a combine, a coach car, an open car, and a caboose, and will take you rain or shine on a ride of 6 scenic miles along the Mississippi River. The train can also be rented for birthday parties.

102 CALVARY CEMETERY
5239 W. Florissant Ave at Union Ave, 63115; (314) 381-1313.
7:30am-5pm, every day.
A map of the cemetery and historical outline are available at the office (8:30am-4:30pm) for self-guided tours.

Calvary Cemetery, established in 1857, contains the graves of many who helped make St. Louis history. To cite a few: Auguste Chouteau, co-founder of the city; J. Mullanphy, one of St. Louis' first millionaries and philanthropists; Alexander McNair, first Governor of Missouri; Archbishops Kenrick and Kain; General Wm. Tecumseh Sherman; Pierre Chouteau; Dred Scott; Tom Dooley; and many others whose names are well known. The memorials within the cemetery are true works of art and architecturally interesting. The silent voices of those sleeping in this cemetery are loudly heard influencing our daily lives. And, Calvary Cemetery is right next to...

103 BELLEFONTAINE CEMETERY
4947 W. Florissant Ave, 63115; (314) 381-0750.
Gates open 8am-5pm, every day.
A map of the cemetery and historical outline are available at the office (M-F, 8am-4:30pm; S, 8-Noon) for self-guided tours.

Bellefontaine Cemetery, established in 1849, when cholera was gripping St. Louis, is a true chronicle of St. Louis history. Many buried here contributed to the westward expansion of our country and the quality of today's life. The trees, many over 100 years old, are of rare beauty. Memorial art of the various periods is interesting and diverse, ranging from that of early American self-taught sculptors who expressed their art in grave markers, to elaborate pieces created by famous architects and sculptors. To cite a few people buried here: Thomas Hart Benton; Dr. Wm. Beaumont; Robert Campbell; General Wm. Clark; James Eads; the Wainwrights; and...the list is long.

104 FAIRGROUNDS PARK
N. Grand Blvd to Fair, Natural Bridge to Kossuth.

In 1855, to de-emphasize the fur trade, Fairgrounds Park became the site of an Agricultural Fair which became an annual Fall event for many years. The popularity of this Fair grew due in a large part to the huge premiums it awarded its exhibitors. The Prince of Wales once participated and 150,000 jammed the Fairgrounds to see him. Fairgrounds Park housed the Zoo until it was moved to Forest Park after the World's Fair, and horse and auto races were tried there for a while.

105 BLACK REPERTORY COMPANY
2240 St. Louis Ave, 63106; (314) 534-3807.

The St. Louis Black Repertory Company, a non-profit organization established in 1976, has become the largest Black performing arts company in Missouri. The "Black Rep", as it has affectionately been nicknamed, presents African-American and Third World theatre and dance productions of rare quality and dynamism. The Company, now in its 15th season, draws both local and out-of-state multi-cultural audiences. It is also committed to an extensive educational program which produces 4-6 touring shows and a Professional Internship Program. The finely selected Black Rep programs are experiences not to be missed.

round St. Louis

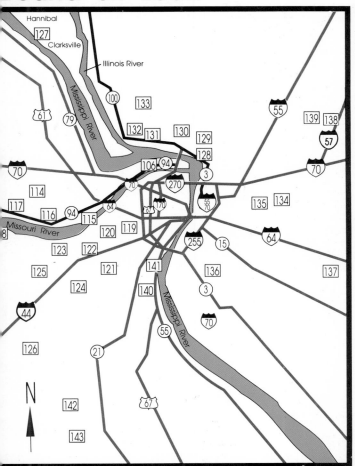

POINTS OF INTEREST
106 St. Charles
114 August A. Busch
 Wildlife Area
115 Katy Trail
116 Defiance
117 Augusta
118 Hermann
119 Lone Elk Park
120 Wolf Sanctuary (Wild
 Canid Survival and
 Research Area)
121 Black Madonna Shrine

122 Wabash, Frisco and
 Pacific Mini-Steam
 Railroad
123 Six Flags
124 Shaw's Arboretum
125 Purina Farms
126 Meramec Caverns
127 Clarksville
128 Great River Rd.
129 Alton
130 Piasa Bird
131 Elsah
132 Twin River Cruise on the
 Belle of Grafton

133 Pere Marquette
 State Park
134 Cahokia Mounds
 Historic Site
135 Fairmount Park Race Track
136 Shrine of Our Lady of
 the Snows
137 Okawville
138 Arcola
139 Rockome Gardens
140 Mastodon State Park
141 Kimmswick
142 Elephant Rocks State Park
143 Johnson's Shut-In's

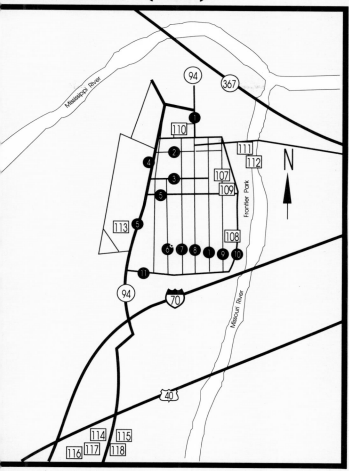

```
POINTS OF INTEREST
107 First Missouri State Capitol
108 Lewis and Clark Center
109 St. Charles Convention and
    Visitors Bureau
110 Academy of the Sacred Heart
111 Goldenrod Showboat
112 Cruises on the Missouri River
113 Lindenwood College
114 August A. Busch Wildlife Area
115 Katy Trail
116 Defiance
117 Augusta
118 Hermann
```

```
STREET
 1 Second St.
 2 Clark
 3 Monroe
 4 Kingshighway
 5 First Capitol Dr.
 6 Fifth St.
 7 Fourth St.
 8 Third St.
 9 Main St.
10 Riverside Dr.
11 Boonslick Rd.
```

GOING WEST

106 ST. CHARLES
22 miles from downtown St. Louis. Access: I-70 W.

St. Charles, the oldest city on the Missouri River, was established by Louis Blanchette in 1769 as a trading post. Lewis joined Clark at St. Charles on May 20, 1804, and on the following day they began their historic exploration to the Pacific Ocean. In 1821, St. Charles became the first capital of the state and remained so until 1826, when the seat of government moved to Jefferson City. Following the publication of a book by Gottfried Duden extolling the similarity of the area to the Rhine Valley, a significant number of Germans immigrated to St. Charles and developed it into a farming, wine, and shipping center. With Mother Duchesne opening the first free school west of the Mississippi in 1818, and the establishment of Lindenwood College in 1827, St. Charles also became an education center. The Frenchtown Historic District restoration reflects how St. Charles has lovingly preserved its rivertown heritage, charm, and hospitality which is made visible through its courtesy trolley transportation and ample parking for visitors. The breezy park along the river is an invitation to walking or enjoying a cruise. St. Charles, with its year-round festivals, seems to create occasions to celebrate life. To name a few of these festivals: the 1st week of Mar sees The Country Peddler Show; 3rd week-end of May, the Lewis and Clark Rendez-vous; 3rd Su of Jun, Music on the Missouri; Jul 1-4, The Riverfest; 3rd week-end of Jul, Jazzfest; 3rd week-end of Aug, Festival of the Little Hills; 2nd week-end of Sept, Bluegrass Festival; 3rd week-end of Sept, Civil War Living History; 1st week-end of Oct, Oktoberfest; 1st week-end of Nov, The Country Peddler Show; Thanksgiving to the end of Dec, Christmas Traditions.

107 FIRST MISSOURI STATE CAPITOL
200-216 S. Main St, St. Charles, MO, 63301; (314) 946-9282.
Open M-S, 10am-4pm; Summer Su, noon-6pm; Winter Su, noon-5pm. Closed Thanksgiving, Dec 25, Jan 1, and Easter. Small admission fee. Tours conducted on the hour.

Honored that their city had been designated a temporary capital in 1821, the citizens of St. Charles provided the 2nd floor of this building to be used as the First Missouri State Capitol and Governor's Office. These facilities were used from 1821 until 1826, when Jefferson City became Missouri's capital. The restored building provides insight into the workings of government at its humble but powerful beginnings; visit the Governor's Office, where 4 Governors served, and the 1st floor of the building where the owner lived and operated a hardware store. There are period furnishings, paintings, early maps of the Missouri Territory, and many interesting items. Adding to the wealth of available information is the new Interpretive Center, which contains graphic and audio-visual displays of early Missouri and St. Charles history.

108 THE LEWIS AND CLARK CENTER
701 Riverside Dr, St. Charles, MO, 63301; (314) 947-3199.
Open all year, 10:30am-4:30pm except Thanksgiving, Dec 25, Jan 1, and Easter.

Recognized by the National Park Service, the Lewis and Clark Center has many hands-on exhibits relating to the 1804 Lewis and Clark Expedition. Dioramas based on daily journals from the Expedition offer a visual interpretation of the Expedition from Wood River, where preparations for the Expedition began, to the Pacific Ocean. Ben York, Clark's constant companion and the first Black man to reach the Pacific Ocean, as well as Sacagawea, a young Shoshone Indian woman instrumental to the success of the Expedition, are also featured. The Center is not only a tourist attraction, but a lively education center for more than 10,000 students and scouts each year.

109 ST. CHARLES CONVENTION & VISITORS BUREAU
210 S. Main St, St. Charles, MO, 63301; (314) 946-7776, or 1-800-366-2427. Open M-F, 8am-5pm; S, 10am-5pm; Su, Noon-5pm.

The St. Charles Convention and Visitors Bureau offers information and maps for self-guided tours.

110 SHRINE OF ST. PHILIPPINE DUCHESNE AND ACADEMY OF THE SACRED HEART
619 N. 2nd St, St. Charles, MO, 63301; (314) 946-6127.
Entrance: 2nd St, turn left onto Decatur, turn left onto Fourth St. Shrine open daily. Voluntary donation may be offered for guided tours which include the historic 1835 school, parlors, and soon-to-be completed Museum. Tour hours: T, Th, F, 9-11am and 1-3pm; S, 10am-Noon and 1-3pm; Su, Noon-3pm.

The Academy of the Sacred Heart in St. Charles, first established by Mother Philippine Duchesne in 1818 in a log cabin, was the first free school west of the Mississippi and the first of many schools conducted by the Religious of the Sacred Heart in America. Visitors will see the room in the convent where she died in 1852. Her tomb is housed in the Shrine. Philippine Duchesne became the 4th United States saint when she was canonized in 1988.

111 GOLDENROD SHOWBOAT
Showboat Landing, St. Charles, MO, 63301; (314) 946-2020.
Open year round. Free Parking.

Built in 1909, the goldenrod Showboat brought entertainment to many a river town in the Midwest and in 1968 was designated a National Historic Landmark. After spending 53 years in St. Louis, and undergoing a facelift, the Goldenrod Showboat now makes St. Charles its home. It offers children's shows, off-Broadway shows, and Dinner-Theatre entertainment.

112 CRUISES ON THE MISSOURI RIVER—SPIRIT OF ST. CHARLES
First Capitol Rd at Frontier Park, St. Charles, MO, 63303; (314) 946-1000 or 1-800-332-3448.
Sightseeing tours daily at 2pm, May-Sept; Apr and Oct, S and Su at 2pm.

Treat yourself to a tour on the Missouri River, or a Dinner Cruise, Moonlight Cruise, a 2-day cruise on the nearby three rivers; the Missouri, Mississippi, and Illinois, with a night's stay at the luxurious Pere Marquette lodge. Entertainment ranges from banjo playing to ragtime music, blues, and gospel music.

113 LINDENWOOD COLLEGE
209 S. Kingshighway, St. Charles, MO, 63301; (314) 949-2000.
Group tours available by calling the Office of Public Relations at 949-4912.

Founded in 1827, Lindenwood College is the 2nd oldest college west of the Mississippi. Sibley Hall, now a women's honors dormitory, was named for founders Mary Easton Sibley and Major George C. Sibley. It is on the National Register of Historic Sites. The Sibley Museum is generally open on M, or by appointment. Artifacts trace the College history to current times. While only briefly noted in James Michener's *Centennial,* the Sibleys played an important role in America's pioneer heritage. Major Sibley established Fort Osage on the Missouri River and helped chart the Santa Fe Trail. Convinced that the country's future rested in education, the Sibleys brought their vision to St. Charles and began their college for women. In 1969, Lindenwood became co-educational and continued its mission toward the development of the whole person through the study of a liberal arts curriculum. The 108-acre, wooded campus holds 7 residence halls, a science building, Jelkyl Theatre for the Performing Arts, a 5,000-seat artificially-turfed stadium with field house, the Harry D. Hendren Gallery in the Fine Arts Building, a student center, a 25,500 watt FM radio station operated by Lindenwood students, plus administrative and faculty offices. The Dorothy Warner Swimming Pool, in Butler Hall, is the first indoor pool west of the Mississippi. The campus is a collegiate inspiration at any time of the year.

114 AUGUST A. BUSCH WILDLIFE AREA
12 miles from St. Charles. I-70/I-40, exit Hwy 94 S. to Hwy D; (314) 441-4554. Winter, open sunrise-7pm; rest of year, sunrise-10pm.

The August A. Busch Wildlife area embraces 6,987 acres with 32 fishing lakes. There are about 70 miles of gravel roads and a 7-mile self-guided auto tour. The wildlife area offers hunting, fishing, sightseeing, educational programs, bird watching, and walks. This is one of the best places to watch the changing fall foliage and flocks of Canada geese.

115 MISSOURI RIVER STATE TRAIL (Katy Trail)
(Weldon Spring to Marthasville Section) 13 miles from St. Charles. Access: Hwy 94 S., exit on Missouri River Trail. For additional information on Katy Trail and Missouri State Park system, call 1-800-334-6946.

In 1986, the Missouri-Kansas-Texas (MKT or "Katy") Railroad decided to cease operation on its route between Machens in northern St. Charles County and Sedalia in Pettis County. This decision presented the chance for an extraordinary recreational opportunity —a 200-mile-long hiking, bicycling, and handicapped-use trail.

The Weldon Spring to Marthasville Section of the Missouri River State Trail comprises a large portion of an eastern pilot section currently under development. The total distance of this section from the U.S. Highway 40-61 bridge at the east boundary of the Weldon Spring Wildlife Area to Marthasville is 26.6 miles.

This section offers a variety of natural and cultural attractions. Limestone bluffs border the trail through the Weldon Spring Wildlife Area. As Augusta is approached from the east, more bluffs appear, this time composed of dolomite and sandstone. The area is rich in biological diversity, with wet lands, and upland and bottomland forests. Wildflowers are abundant, and the trail is ideal for bird watching. The Missouri River State Trail has been designed specifically for bicyclists and hikers. Wheelchairs are allowed; no other motorized vehicles, except official and emergency vehicles, are allowed. No hunting or discharging of firearms is allowed. All state park rules apply and are posted at trail heads. The trail is open only during daylight hours.

116 HISTORIC DANIEL BOONE HOME (Defiance, MO)
20 miles from St. Charles.
Access: Hwy 94 south to Hwy F, Defiance, MO, 63341; (314) 987-2221. Open mid-Mar through mid-Dec, every day, 9am-7pm; and mid-Dec through mid-Mar, S and Su, 11am-4pm. Small admission fee.

One of our most famous Americans who played an important part in the development of Missouri's history and in the early history of St. Charles County is the frontiersman, Daniel Boone. In 1798, Daniel Boone was invited by Spain to settle in the Missouri Territory, which at that time was under Spanish rule and part of the vast Louisiana Territory. He left Kentucky in 1799 with his family and approximately 50 others to claim and farm the land. In 1800, Boone was appointed Magistrate of the Missouri Territory and held court under the famous Judgment Tree, which stood close to the Georgian-style home built of native quarried limestone during the years 1803-1810 by Daniel and his son, Nathan. Boone, an industrious master craftsman, created the woodwork which may still be seen in the home. Daniel Boone died in 1820 at the age of 86 in the small northwest bed chamber on the main floor. The Historic Daniel Boone Home, listed on the National Register, contains furnishings of the period, many of which are Boone family heirlooms. Boonesfield Village, which will be situated on the Boone estate, will be the basis of a living history village consisting of 30-35 meticulously restored structures dating back to the early 1800s. Tradesmen of the period will demonstrate their trade for the public...a living, educational, hands-on experience for those of all ages.

MISSOURI WINERIES

There are more than 30 wineries in Missouri, 11 of them within a short distance of St. Charles, in the scenic Missouri River Valley. Missouri wines since their development have received national and international awards. In the late 1800s, Missouri played a significant role in saving the phyllexora-infected vineyards of Montpellier, France, by sending them stock roots. Two statues in Montpellier commemorate this saving of the vineyards of the Old World by the vines of the New. A list of wineries within a short distance of St. Charles open to the public for samplings, tours, and purchases, follows:

Winery of the Little Hills
501 S. Main St
St. Charles, MO 63301
(314) 946-9339

Boone Country Winery
125 Boone Country Ln
Defiance, MO 63341
(314) 987-2400

Montelle Winery at Osage Ridge
PO Box 147
Augusta, MO 63332
(314) 228-4464

Augusta Winery
PO Box 8
Augusta, MO 63332
(314) 228-4301

Mount Pleasant Winery
5634 High St
Augusta, MO 63332
(314) 228-4419

Blumenhof Vineyards
PO Box 30
Dutzow, MO 63342
(314) 433-2245

Stone Hill Wine Co.
North Outer Rd
New Florence, MO 63363
(314) 835-2420

Bias Vineyard and Wines
Rt 1
Berger, MO 63014
(314) 834-5475

Stone Hill Winery
Rt 1, Box 26
Hermann, MO 65041
(314) 486-2120

Hermannhof Winery
330 E. 1st St
Hermann, MO 65041
(314) 486-5959

Adam Puchta Winery
Box 73 Rt 1
Hermann, MO 65041
(314) 486-5596 or 486-2361

For more information on wineries, call 1-800-392-WINE

117 AUGUSTA

Augusta is home to 3 wineries open year round, Mount Pleasant Montelle, and Augusta; the town is delightful, with quaint wood and antique shops, bakeries, and Bed and Breakfast accommodations.

118 HERMANN

80 miles west of St. Louis.
Access: I-94 S., Hwy 100 S. or: I-70 W., Hwy 100 S.

Hermann was settled in 1836 by a community of "idealist" German immigrants who were intent on creating in the New World a city where German culture could flourish. Hermann became known as the Missouri Rhineland, or a "Bit of Germany Close to Home". A wine industry developed in this Missouri Valley town, which gave Hermann 4 wineries: Stone Hill Winery, Hermannhof Winery, Adam Puchta Winery, and Bias Winery (9 miles from Hermann), which today compete in world markets. The wineries are open year round for tours and wine, cheese, and sausage samplings. Hospitality of the Old World can be experienced at 19 Bed and Breakfasts and at the many restaurants of the area which specialize in delicious German food. The visitor can be entertained and delightfully impressed by the talents displayed at the Show Boat Community Theatre, with performances on selected W, and festival week-ends, Apr-Oct.

HERMANN VISITOR INFORMATION CENTER
306 Market St, Hermann, MO, 65041; (314) 486-2744.

Be sure to stop in for maps, tours, and invaluable information regarding Hermann and its surrounding area.

HISTORIC HERMANN MUSEUM
4th at Schiller St; (314) 486-2017 or 486-2781.

This old German School, built in 1871, was used as an elementary school until 1955. Today it houses a most interesting Craft Shop on the 1st floor, and on the 2nd, the Historic Hermann Museum, which, with the Heritage Room, the Els Room, and River Room, resurrects Hermann's past.

DEUTSCHHEIM STATE HISTORIC SITE
109 W. Second St, includes 2 historic houses: the Pommer-Gentner House, and the Strehly House. Tours can be arranged at the West 2nd St office or by calling (314) 486-2200.

WHISKEY JACK'S MUSEUM
127 E. 4th St; (314) 486-2871.

Whiskey Jack's Museum has the largest collection of memorabilia depicting one of America's most colorful eras, Prohibition.

HERMANN FESTIVALS

Hermann has many festivals throughout the year. To cite a few; the Fasching Ball, in Feb; the Wurstfest, 3rd week-end in Mar; The Maifest, 3rd week-end in May; the Annual Antique Market, 3rd week-end in Jun; the Great Stone Hill Grape Stomp, 2nd S in Aug; the Volksmarch, 3rd week-end in Sept; the Octoberfest, every week-end in Oct; an Old-Fashioned Christmas, in Dec.

GOING SOUTHWEST

119 LONE ELK PARK
25 miles from St. Louis.
Access: I-44, exit Valley Park, N. Outer Rd W.; (314) 889-3208.
Free Admission. Stop at visitors' center for guidance.

Lone Elk Park provides a good example of the hilly terrain surrounding the Meramec Valley. The park, a wildlife area, is designed for drives through densely wooded hills. Observe at close range the bison, elk, and deer freely roaming the park.

120 WOLF SANCTUARY
(Wild Canid Survival and Research Center)
28 miles from St. Louis. Located at Tyson Research Center, Eureka, MO 63025; (314) 938-5900.
Access: I-44, Beaumont-Antire Rd exit, turn right. 2 weeks advance reservation required for all programs offered except Open House Day, 1st Su of Oct. Call for reservation, M-F, 9am-5pm. Admission fee. Group Tours or Program-Tours conducted every-day, 9am-4pm, except W; Small Group Tours conducted 1st S of month, 10-11am; and Small Group Program-Tours conducted 3rd S of month, 1-3pm; Wolf Howls, T and F, 7:30pm, Sept 21-mid-Dec; Campfires, S, 8pm, Sept-Dec.

This visit you will never forget! The threat of extinction plaguing the wolf led Marlin Perkins and his friends to create the Wolf Sanctuary in 1971. A visit to the Sanctuary offers an opportunity to see a variety of rare wolves; Tundra wolves, Red wolves, Timber wolves, Iranian wolves, and 11 of the only 38 Mexican wolves in captivity in the world. The program hopes to educate the public and eventually return the wolves to the wild where they belong.

121 BLACK MADONNA SHRINE
35 miles from St. Louis. Eureka, MO, 63025; (314) 938-5361.
Access: I-44, Eureka exit, 8 miles on County W to County FF. Open daily, 8am-8pm. Free admission.

The shrine, built over a period of 22 years by Br. Bronislaus to honor the Black Madonna of his native Poland, consists of several grottos creatively constructed with barite stone, costume jewelry, sea shells, and fragments of glass. Garden and picnic facilities close to the grounds.

122 WABASH, FRISCO AND PACIFIC MINI-STEAM RAILROAD
32 miles from downtown. Glencoe, MO 63038; (314) 1-587-3538.
Access: I-44, Eureka exit No. 264, turn to right, 3½ miles N. on Hwy 109, right onto Old State Rd, then 2nd right onto Washington-

Grand Aves, and continue ½ mile to the Station. Open only on Su. 1st Su of May through last Su of Oct, 1-4:15pm. Small fee; children under 3 free.

The Wabash, Frisco and Pacific Mini-Steam Railroad was originally located at Natural Bridge and Brown Rds in North County in 1939. A group of railroad enthusiasts trying to preserve the memory of steam-powered passenger trains operates real steam locomotives which provide a 2-mile round-trip ride along the scenic Meramec River. A good chance to bring out the child in all of us. For further information or photo brochure, send SASE to: W F and P, 1569 Villa Angela Ln, Hazelwood, MO 63042-1630.

123 SIX FLAGS OVER MID-AMERICA

25 miles southwest of St. Louis on I-44, Allenton exit. Eureka, MO 63025; (314)938-5300. Open every day from May 23 through Sept; week-ends only from Apr 8 through May 21 and Sept 9 through Oct 29. Discount for senior citizens. Free wheelchairs available for returnable deposit. Hours: Daily, 10am-10pm except F, 10am-Midnight.

Six Flags over Mid-America is an amusement park for all the young at heart. There are shows, music, attractions, and more than 100 rides. Two main productions are held in the Palace and in Miss Kitty's Saloon. Periodically, The Old Glory Theater features name entertainers. There are 3 roller coasters sure to delight the enthusiasts: the unparalleled Screaming Eagle wooden coaster, famed for its deep drops, careens at speeds up to 70 miles per hour; the steel coaster, the Ninja, the black belt of roller coasters, turns head over heels with its loops and corkscrew turns; and the Mine Train, which travels through simulated mine tunnels. Dancing in the Tremor Pavilion, 7-10pm to video music. Country Fairs, contests, and other events are also held week-ends, Sept through Oct.

124 SHAW'S ARBORETUM

35 miles southwest of St. Louis.
Access: I-44, Gray Summit exit, left to Hwy 100 W., right onto 100, to the main entrance of the Arboretum; (314)742-3512. Admission fee. Register at Visitors' Center. Open all year, 7am-sunset, except 1 week in Nov, which is deer season.

The Arboretum, an extension of the Missouri Botanical Garden, is a nature reserve of 2,400 acres with 12 miles of hiking trails, woodlands, a restored prairie, and wildlife. The Meramec River flows through the property, and river trails lead to it. Educational programs for adults and children are available.

125 PURINA FARMS

42 miles from downtown.
Access: I-44, Gray Summit exit, N. on Hwy 100 for ½ mile, left on MM; (314) 982-3232.
Mid-Mar through mid-Nov. Spring and Fall, open W-Su; weekdays, 9:30am-1pm; week-ends, 9:30am-3pm. Summer, T-Su; 9:30am-3pm. Free admission. Reservations Required.

A visit to the Purina Farms in the scenic Meramec Valley is a relaxing and educational outing which appeals to people of all ages. Purina Farms explores the special role pets and domestic farm animals play in our lives. Surrounded by nearly 1,600 acres of farm land, Purina Farms features live domestic animals, educational graphic displays, videos and hands-on activities. Demonstrations on dog obedience, pet grooming, cow milking, and sheep herding are scheduled daily (weather permitting), along with wagon rides in the parking lot.

126 MERAMEC CAVERNS

60 miles from St. Louis. Stanton, MO, 63079; (314) 468-3166.
Access: I-44, exit 230, 3 miles S. on Hwy W. Open daily, 9am-5pm all year. Closed Thanksgiving and Dec 25. Admission fee. Walking Tours conducted every half hour.

Missouri is a state of caves. So far, 5,000 caves have been discovered, including a large number in St. Louis. Meramec Caverns, discovered in 1720 and first used as a show cave in 1933, is one of the most popular and scenic show caves in the United States. Meramec Caverns has 5 levels, spectacular stalagmite formations, and an enormous 3,000-seat chamber which has been used for balls and parties. Historically, caves have been used for many purposes: as living quarters for pre-historic Indians; as hideouts to avoid conscription, the law, and slavery; as storage and refrigeration areas; as mushroom farms; and as meeting rooms and places of entertainment (beer gardens, ballroom dancing, theatres). The Meramec Caverns are no exception, having been used during the Civil War as a station for the underground railroad through which many slaves escaped to the North; as a hideout for Jesse James; and as a location for filming segments of the movies *Lassie* and *Tom Sawyer*.

GOING NORTH

127 CLARKSVILLE

70 miles from St. Louis.
Access: I-70 W, Hwy 79 N. The Skyride on Hwy 79 is open M-F,
9:30am-5:30pm; S-Su, 9:30am-7pm, Memorial-Labor Day; and
week-ends in May, Sept, and Oct. Admission fee. (314) 242-3711.

The highest bluff between St. Paul and New Orleans, is located in Clarksville. A skyride takes visitors to a 600-foot lookout point which commands a breathtaking view of 800 square miles and the Mighty Mississippi. The town, full of ante-bellum homes and interesting shops, is also known as Appletown, for its many apple orchards. The Applefest Festival is held during the 2nd week-end of Oct and Eagle Days, celebrating the many bald eagles gathering in the winter, are held the last week-end of Jan.

GOING NORTHEAST

128 GREAT RIVER ROAD

30 minutes from downtown.
Access: from I-70 W., exit Riverview Blvd, Hwy 367 N. to Alton,
Great River Road W. From I-270, Exit Hwy 367 N. to Alton. Great
River Road W.

Not to be missed! Located in Illinois about 30 minutes from downtown St. Louis, The Great River Road provides a spectacular ride for 35 miles along the Mississippi River and its bluffs. This stretch, which includes Alton, Piasa Creek, Elsah, Grafton, and Pere Marquette State Park, unfolds one of the most scenic and majestic views of the river. Visitors with time to spare can extend their trip to Kampsville, 35 miles past Pere Marquette on Hwy 100 and visit the Kampsville Archeological Museum. Those curious to see the Mississippi-Missouri confluence and Lock and Dam No. 26 in operation can continue past Alton east on The Great River Road (also known as Route 100, 3, and 143).

129 ALTON, ILLINOIS

25 miles from St. Louis.
Access: from I-70 W., exit Riverview Blvd, Hwy 367 N. to Alton,
Great River Road W. From I-270, exit Hwy 367 N. to Alton, Great
River Road W.

Alton, established in 1817, was a very significant riverport. It was in Alton that the Eagle Packets, which were used to transport cotton and other goods on the river, were constructed. The Melvin Price Lock and Dam 26 can be seen in full operation at the Alton Riverfront. There is a 110-foot monument dedicated to Elijah Lovejoy, one of the first clergymen to serve Des Peres Presbyterian Church in St. Louis, who moved to Alton and continued his work with the Underground Railroad to help Blacks escape to freedom. The many old homes and over 60 antique stores attract many visitors to Alton. The Greater Alton area offers 16 public or private golf courses, including Illinois' only public Arnold Palmer-designed and managed golf course. Riverboat Gambling in beautiful surroundings while cruising the most scenic part of the Mississippi River is available. For more information, visit or call:

THE GREATER ALTON TWIN RIVERS / CONVENTION AND VISITORS BUREAU
200 Piasa St, Alton, IL, 62001; 1-800-ALTONIL.
M-F, 8:30am-4:30pm; S and Su, 9am-4:30pm, year round except Thanksgiving, Dec 25, Jan 1, and Jan week-ends.

THE ALTON MUSEUM OF HISTORY AND ART
121 E. Broadway, Alton, IL, 62002; (618) 462-2763; T-S, 10am-4pm. Closed Jan and holidays. Free admission.
    The Alton Museum of History and Art reflects the soul of this once-bustling rivertown whose character was shaped by the Indians, the river, explorers, and boat builders. The gallery exhibits of local artists are done with such flair that following exhibits are always anticipated. Colorful history is reflected by the exhibits in: The Piasa Room, which explains the Illini Indian painting on Alton Bluff and the legend attached to it; The Four River Room, which depicts the river as the lifeline of the region; The Lincoln Room, which unveils the little-known Lincoln-Shields duel in 1842 near Alton, and the Lincoln-Douglas debate held a block away from the museum; and The Alton Room, which unfolds the industrial past of Alton, its breweries, railroads, milling, packet, and glass companies. On another floor are Lovejoy's Print Shop, whose anti-slavery articles made him the first martyr for the freedom of the press, and memorabilia of Robert Wadlow, Alton's 8'11" citizen, the world's tallest man. A most hospitable and entertaining museum!

130 PIASA BIRD
    Along the Great River Road, 5.5 miles out of Alton, is the Piasa bird facsimile. Marquette's journal, written in 1693, reports that near the Mississippi-Missouri confluence, he and Joliet saw paintings on the bluffs of a bird-like monster which, he admits, frightened them at first. The Illini Indians' "Piasa Bird" legends revolve around the central theme that many thousands of moons ago, when mastodons roamed the land, there existed a bird-like creature which craved human flesh. Though the original Piasa bird has long ago faded, a facsimile can still be seen along the Great River Road near Alton.

131 ELSAH

10 miles from Alton.
Access: I-270, Hwy 367 to Alton, IL, Great River Road, Elsah, IL.

Elsah is a quaint village with homes of various styles dating to the late 1800s. Elsah's Landing Restaurant, the only one in town, features excellent home-cooked meals, breads, cakes, soups, and pies. The village also has several beautiful Bed and Breakfasts. The entire village is on the National Registry of Historic Places.

132 TWIN RIVERS CRUISE ON THE BELLE OF GRAFTON

501 E. Front St, Grafton, IL, 62037; (618) 786-2318.
Open May 15-Nov 15. Cruises M-F, 2pm; S-Su, Noon, 2, 4pm; F, Moonlight Cruise, 8:30-11pm; S, Dinner Cruise, 7-10pm; Bar and snacks available. Occasionally live entertainment with Dinner Cruise.

Come aboard! The Belle of Grafton, a 65-foot paddlewheeler replica, sails on spectacular sections of the Mississippi and Illinois Rivers bordered by towering bluffs. An impressive sight anytime, particularly when autumn leaves turn to red and gold.

133 PERE MARQUETTE STATE PARK

About 45 miles from St. Louis and 12 miles from Alton.
Access: I-270, Hwy 367 N. to Pere Marquette. Open all year; (618) 786-2331. Hotel and restaurant reservation advisable.

Named in memory of Pere Marquette, one of the first 2 Europeans to map the Mississippi River. A massive rustic lodge located in Pere Marquette State Park faces the Illinois River. Recently facelifted, the lodge offers rooms in the hotel, cabins nestled in the wooded park, and dining accommodations. There are hiking trails and picnic areas, and a good spot to watch the bald eagles on the bluff.

GOING EAST

134 CAHOKIA MOUNDS HISTORIC SITE AND INTERPRETIVE CENTER

8 miles from downtown St. Louis. Box 681, Collinsville, IL, 62234; (618) 346-5160. Access: from downtown, Popular St Bridge, east on I-55-70, Route 111 exit 6, right to light, left on Collinsville Rd. From I-270: 270 east, across the Chain of Rocks Bridge, 255 south to exit 24 Collinsville Rd, left on Collinsville Rd, 2 miles; about 13 miles from the Chain of Rocks Bridge. Historic site open daily, 8am-dusk except Thanksgiving, Dec 25, Jan 1. Interpretive Center open daily, 9am-5pm except Thanksgiving, Dec 25, Jan 1. Free admission. Self-guided tours; seasonal guided tours. Special events.

This excursion is a must! Archeological finds have shown that the most sophisticated pre-historic Indian civilization lived in the Cahokia area from 700 to 1500 A.D. and vanished before the Europeans came. Cahokia is considered the largest pre-historic Indian center in America; its population at one time reached the 20,000 mark. This site, so essential to our understanding of the pre-history of North America, was designated by the United Nations a World Heritage site in 1982. The Interpretive Center has a life-size reproduction of a Mississippian village and provides invaluable information on this culture, displays of chipped stones, arrowheads, drills, spades, sea shells, hoes, picks, pottery, knives, and sun calendars found at Cahokia. The orientation movie and the walking tours of the Mounds are outstanding, Heritage America, the special event of the year, with Native Americans from across the country, activities and demonstrations, is held Sept 27-29 in the Central Plaza. Call for other events.

135 FAIRMOUNT PARK RACE TRACK

8 miles from the Arch. Fairmount Park, Collinsville, IL, 62234; (314) 436-1516.
Access: Poplar St Bridge, I-55/70 E., Black Lane exit 9, left onto Collinsville Rd. Open year round T at 1:30pm; W-S, 7:30pm.

Thoroughbred racing Mar-Nov; Nov-Mar, harness racing. A restaurant on the grounds. The special event of the year is the Fairmount Derby held in the summer.

136 NATIONAL SHRINE OF OUR LADY OF THE SNOWS

10 miles from downtown St. Louis. 9500 West Illinois, Rt 15, Belleville, IL, 62223; (314) 241-3400 or (618) 397-6700.
Access from downtown: Poplar St Bridge, I-55/70, I-64 east, I-255 south, IL Rt 15 east, exit 17A. Open daily, 8am-10pm. Guided tram tours at 9:25am and 1pm. Free admission.

The National Shrine of Our Lady of the Snows is the largest and most contemporary outdoor Shrine in the United States; it offers a unique experience of peace and beauty. The visitor will find on these 200 acres of superbly landscaped hills, a comfortable motel, a restaurant, a 3,500-seat open-air amphitheater, an outdoor Way of the Cross, a replica of the Lourdes Grotto, a Mother's and Father's prayer garden, chapels, and all sorts of interesting people, activities, and events. People of all faiths from all over the world come here to visit. The Guild Center features a multi-media presentation from creation to redemption which is well worth seeing. However long the stay, the visitor is sure to emerge refreshed and renewed. The gentle bell chimes ringing on the hour and occasional views of the St. Louis downtown skyline sifting through the trees are the only reminders of citylife at large. "The Way of Lights" Christmas display draws people from far away to experience anew the wonder and magic of that night.

137 OKAWVILLE

40 miles from downtown St. Louis. The Original Springs Hotel, 506 Hanover St, Okawville, IL, 62271; (618) 243-5458 or 1-800-842-1867.

Access: I-64 E., exit 41. Bathhouses, Su, M, T, Th, 9am-5pm; W, F, S, 9am-8pm. Admission fee.

"The Original Springs Hotel" was constructed in 1867 after mineral springs were discovered in Okawville and found to have qualities similar to those of the famous Baden-Baden Spa in Germany. Situated in the heart of a town that seems to have stood still during the march of time, this quaint, century-old hotel and restaurant, recently renovated, offers mineral bath facilities and massages. While in Okawville, the visitor can experience Heritage House Museum, an unrestored turn-of-the century home, harness shop, and commercial laundry.

138 ARCOLA

80 miles from St. Louis.

Access: I-70 E. to Effingham, 57 N. to Arcola, IL. Turn left, follow signs to Rockome Gardens.

Get away and spend a day with the Amish! Arcola and its environs, settled by the Amish, have withstood changing times for over 100 years. Once a farming community, the Amish have turned to other ways to make a living, such as making furniture, harness, and buggies, and operating restaurants which, as with everything they do, show art and love. It is a charming town where past and present meet everywhere, but most visibly on the highways, where yesteryear's buggies travel next to today's cars, a mesmerizing sight. A good place to start a visit is at Rockome Gardens.

139 ROCKOME GARDENS

80 miles from St. Louis
Access: I-70 E. to Effingham, 57 N. to Arcola, IL. Turn left, follow signs to Rockome Gardens; (217) 268-4216.

Rockome Gardens contains unusual groupings of rock-fencing, gates, and attractive displays of flowers. There is an Amish furniture shop, restaurant, bakery shop, a carriage house, a livery stable, a blacksmith shop, a candy shop, a craft shop, a trading post, and many more things to see and do. It is a good place to see and understand the Amish ways of life. There are many books in the gift shop which are sure to provide answers to all the questions you ever wanted to ask about the Amish. Special events attract people from afar: the annual Indian Pow Wow Festival on Memorial Day week-end; the famous Arcola Broom Corn Festival during the 2nd week of Sept; the Annual Rockome Gardens Quilt Show, 1st through 3rd weeks of Jul; Kids' Day, 1st week of Aug; and many others. For more information, write: Arcola Chamber of Commerce, P.O. Box 274, Arcola, IL, 61910.

49

BERART GALLERY

W OPEN SATURDAY 12 TO 4

50

51

GOING SOUTH

140 MASTODON STATE PARK
20 miles south of St. Louis. Access: I-55 S., Imperial-Kimmswick exit; (314) 464-2976. Museum hours: 8am-4:30pm, M-S; Noon-4:30pm, Su. Open all year.

Remains of mastodons were first discovered in Kimmswick, MO, in the 1800s by Dr. Albert C. Koch, who later unearthed one large mastodon skeleton now on exhibit at the British Museum of National History. In 1979, the finding of Clovis spears embedded within mastodon bones provided the first concrete evidence that man hunted mastodons during the Ice Age and linked the man to the Clovis culture. To find human remains at Mastodon Park would cast light on America's first men, a discovery which would be of national importance. These finds make Mastodon Park one of the most significant sites in North America today for the study of men and animals of the Ice Age. Visitors are invited to see the museum in the park and watch archeologists when excavations are in progress. The park museum's various exhibits include a life-size replica of a mastodon skeleton, Clovis-type spear points 12,000 years old, tusks 17,500 years old, and carbon 14-tested mastodon bones indicating that these elephant-like mammals still roamed Missouri 8,000 years ago. While at the park, plan on hiking or having a picnic. Don't fear, mastodons have long become extinct; why, is still the puzzle. While at Mastodon State Park, right across the highway is...

141 KIMMSWICK
23 miles south of St. Louis.
Access: I-55 S., Imperial-Kimmswick exit, left onto Hwy 61-67, right ½ block, turn left on K to Kimmswick. Shops closed M.

Founded in 1859 by Theodore Kimm, Kimmswick grew to be a prosperous German community. Kimmswick's once-popular Mineral Springs and Montesano Park Resort attracted St. Louisans who came to Kimmswick by steamer and railroad. Kimmswick has retained the quaintness and charm of a small rivertown and its easy-going pace; restaurants and specialty and antique shops offer everyone an escape from the city.

142 ELEPHANT ROCKS STATE PARK
80 miles from St. Louis.
Access: I-55 S., Hwy 21, at the northwest edge of Graniteville on Hwy 21 in Iron County; (314) 697-5395.

Elephant Rocks State Park has the most puzzling geological formations in Missouri. The 129-acre park contains a large number of massive granite rocks over a billion years old. Because of their size and shape, these rocks are referred to as elephants. Dumbo, one of the largest rocks in the park, is 27 feet tall, 35 feet long, 17 feet wide, and estimated to weigh 680 tons. Outside the park is one of the oldest quarries in Missouri; it provided stone for the Eads Bridge and streets of St. Louis. The park offers something for all members of the family: shaded picnic areas, paved trails for wheelchairs, a one-mile Braille trail for the visually impaired, and many rocks to explore.

143 JOHNSON'S SHUT-INS STATE PARK

80 miles from St. Louis.
Access: I-55 S., south on Hwy 21, 8 miles north of Lesterville on Reynolds County N.; (314) 546-2450.

Johnson's Shut-Ins State Park, a 2,990-acre park, is located in the scenic St. Francois Mountains. The swift waters of the Black River flow through the rocky gorges or "shut-ins" formed by volcanic eruptions more than 1.5 billion years ago. The Shut-Ins Trail, a 2.5-mile loop, provides access to the park. The park has camping, hiking, and breathtaking wilderness scenery of presettlement times. In certain areas, the shut-ins form pools among smooth volcanic rocks where swimming is allowed.

PARKS

There are many Parks throughout the area: City, County, and State Parks. For more information, call City Parks at (314) 535-1503, County Parks at (314) 889-2863, and State Parks at 1-800-334-6946.

There are 46 State Parks, 28 Historic Sites, and 1 State Recreational Trail. For more information regarding boating, float trips, canoeing, etc., call 1-800-334-6946, or write Missouri Division of Tourism, Box 1055, Jefferson City, MO, 65102.

52

53

54

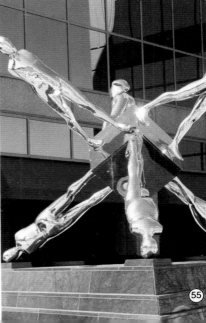

55

ETHNIC GROUPS AND FESTIVALS

The fabric of St. Louis society has been enriched by an influx of ethnic groups from around the world. For the benefit of visitors or newcomers to St. Louis, a few of these ethnic groups have been listed here as well as some of the colorful festivals and annual events they offer at various times of the year.

ALLIANCE FRANCAISE OF ST. LOUIS
8505 Delmar Blvd, 63124; (314) 432-0734.

The Alliance Francaise, an international non-profit organization, established in St. Louis in 1903, complements the city's strong French heritage by promoting an appreciation of French culture through the French language, lectures, performing arts, student exchanges, and social events. The Alliance sponsors annual benefit balls, the Traditional Fete des Rois in Jan, Bastille Day fetes on Jul 14th, excursions to Ste. Genevieve, trips to La Belle France, sing alongs, poetry readings, lectures on France and French life, travel slide shows, games, contests, and French films followed by discussion.

AMERICAN-HELLENIC EDUCATIONAL PROGRESSIVE ASSOCIATION (AHEPA)
5840 Oakland Ave, 63110; (314) 647-8910.

The American-Hellenic Educational Progressive Association in St. Louis is a branch of a National Greek Organization. The organization was established in the 1920s to help Greek immigrants obtain United States citizenship and become integral members of American society. AHEPA has now become an international organization consisting of 498 chapters, 15,000 members of which are in the St. Louis area. Their annual events are the May Festival, the Annual Valentine Dance, and the Greek Festival in Sept.

ANCIENT ORDER OF HIBERNIANS
Hibernian Hall, 3301 Magnolia St; (314) 776-9090.

The Ancient Order of Hibernians, the oldest Irish fraternal organization in St. Louis, pursues goals of friendship, unity, and Christian charity. The AOH is very active in all Irish affairs, social and traditional, in the metropolitan area. The Hibernians hold a parade each year on St. Patrick's Day.

AUSTRALIAN-AMERICAN CHAMBER OF COMMERCE OF ST. LOUIS (AACC)
1 Mercantile Center, Suite 3400, 63101; (314) 342-1649.

The Australian-American Chamber of Commerce of St. Louis is an organization designed to foster business, cultural, educational, and social links between Australia and the United States. The

AACC holds many interesting programs through the year, including Australia Week in Sept-Oct, and an Australia Day Celebration on Jan 26.

CHINESE COMMUNITY IN THE GREATER ST. LOUIS AREA

For information regarding Chinese events, call the Chinese Cultural Center; (314) 567-5540.

The Chinese Community of St. Louis, established in 1850, now has 30,000 members representing Chinese-Americans born and raised in the United States and Chinese emigrants of more than 20 Chinese Provinces (including Taiwan) in the eastern half of China with a geographic area about half the size of the U.S. The Chinese community is reinforced by ethnic-Chinese people from Malaysia, Indonesia, Singapore, the Philippines, Vietnam, and Korea. Most of these are professionals practicing in all segments of society, or entrepreneurs engaged in the food industry, import-export, newspaper, printing, and retail businesses. The large diversity of the Community has given rise to numerous religious, social, cultural, and educational organizations, and one political organization, The Organization of Chinese Americans, St. Louis Chapter (OCA-St. Louis), solely devoted to encourage Chinese-Americans to join in the American mainstream and political process. The Society welcomes all visitors to its diverse cultural events, food sales, exhibits, dances, and offerings of music, opera, and martial arts, frequently presented at the VP Fair, International Folklore Festival, and at the University of Missouri-St. Louis, Washington University, and St. Louis University. The main event of the year is the much-looked-for Chinese New Year, celebrated between Jan 20th and Feb 20th, depending on the arrangement in the lunar calendar.

COLOMBIAN SOCIETY

102 Pebblebrook Ct, 63146; (314) 567-4762.

The Colombian Society of St. Louis, founded in 1985, provides social gatherings to Colombians. The musical talent of many of the society members provides colorful and joyful programs for its members not to mention the warm hospitality they extend to all those interested in their heritage. Their annual event is Independence Day, celebrated on the week-end following Jul 20th.

DEN DANSKE CLUB, THE DANISH CLUB

655 Hurstgreen Rd, 63119; (314) 962-2730.

The Den Danske Club of St. Louis is primarily a social organization which provides St. Louis Danes and friends of Danes an opportunity to socialize. Membership is open to those interested in the Danish heritage. The club's social programs include many events such as picnics, bonfires, dinners, and Scandinavian Folk Dances. Main annual events are the Skt Hansaften celebration on

Jun 23, the Scandinavian Picnic in the Fall, and the Christmas party.

FILIPINO-AMERICAN SOCIETY
808 Wenneker, 63124; (314) 863-8809.

The Filipino-American Society was established to promote Filipino-American relations through cultural, social, and charitable programs. The Society welcomes visitors to the unique events, dances, and shows it sponsors and participates annually in the International Folklore Festival. The Society contributes annually to the 100 Neediest Cases and to the relief of disaster-struck areas.

GERMAN CULTURAL SOCIETY
3652 S. Jefferson Ave, 63118; (314) 771-8368.

The German Emigrant Societies have always been active in St. Louis and played a major role in the city's development, especially by helping newcomers to become settled. The Germans' love of music gave St. Louis many bands and singing and dancing groups. The German-American organizations are still very active, designed to preserve and advance the German culture. The German Cultural Society, one of the largest German societies in St. Louis, with many members from Eastern European countries, welcomes everyone to their annual events.

INDIA ASSOCIATION OF ST. LOUIS
PO Box 607, Chesterfield, MO, 63006; (314) 432-6888 or 892-5991.

The India Association of St. Louis, begun in 1954 by Indian university students, has grown to 7,500 members who contribute their professional expertise to the St. Louis Community. Created to preserve the Indian cultural heritage, the Association has shared the Indian culture with others through its many social programs. The Mahatma Gandhi Center, the India Association's center, welcomes everyone to its many social programs and 3 annual festivals: The Spring Harvest Festival, "Holi" or festival of colors, in late Mar or early Apr; the "Mela Festival" in the 2nd week of Aug; and the Festival of Lights, "Deepawali", in the 2nd or 3rd week of Nov. After many years in planning, India Association now has a Hindu Temple. Each Oct, Asha Prem's innovative productions of the traditional Dances of India, subtly choreographed for Western audiences, brings with cymbals, foot rhythms, bells and hand gestures, the beauty and energy of Hindu dances. (314) 997-0911.

INTERNATIONAL FOLKLORE FEDERATION
2 Robindale Dr, 63124; (314) 997-1445 or 921-1192.

The International Folklore Association represents more than 40 groups of various nationalities offering cultural exchange programs between Americans and other nationalities and promoting understanding of other cultures. The International Folklore Festival is held at the end of May through the beginning of Jun.

ITALIA-AMERICA BOCCE CLUB
5627 Manchester Ave, 63110; (314) 645-9781.

The Italia-America Bocce Club of St. Louis maintains one of the finest Bocce courts in America. The game, introduced in America by Italian immigrants, has gained popularity in the U.S. and recognition from the International Olympic Committee. The Italia-America Bocce members participate in yearly tournaments and occasionally host the United States Bocce Federation National Championship Tournament.

JEWISH COMMUNITY CENTERS ASSOCIATION (JCCA)
2 Millstone Campus Dr, 63146; (314) 432-5700.

The Jewish Community Center Association, or JCCA, as it is referred to in St. Louis, is one place where people of all backgrounds can socialize, learn, and relax in a Jewish environment. The Association offers many cultural arts programs, classes, theatre performances, Israeli cultural programs, physical education, family programs, and group services. The Association features annual events such as The Jewish Folklore Festival in the Summer, the Jewish Folk Art Festival in Sept, and the Jewish Book Festival in the first week of Nov. The JCCA film series in Yiddish, Russian, and English is one of its many exciting cultural programs.

MEXICAN SOCIETY OF BENITO JUAREZ OF ST LOUIS
4200 N. 20th St, 63107; (314) 739-2243 or the Mexican Consulate, 436-3233.

The Mexican Society of Benito Juarez was established in 1936 to preserve and pass on the customs, traditions, and cultural treasures of the Mexican heritage to the children. Several cultural programs, art exhibits, folklore and historic presentations are offered in the area, many with the International Folklore Federation of St. Louis. The Society's own artistic group sponsors musical education with an accent on Mexican music, and charitable activities for humanitarian causes. The Society offers 2 annual scholarships to children of its members. Annual events include 2 Dances: The Cinco de Mayo, Battle of Puebla, on May 5; and Independence Day, on the 15th of Sept.

PERUVIAN SOCIETY OF ST. LOUIS
515 Medina Dr, 63122; (314) 966-0401.

Welcoming everyone, the goal of the Peruvian Society of St. Louis is to preserve its heritage and, through its social and cultural activities, share its heritage. Activities include lectures, presentation of authors, and movies. The Society's programs and annual events include: Independence Day, celebrated on the week-end following Jul 28th; Mardi Gras Carnival Party, just before Lent; and The Friendship Luncheon in Oct, which calls for all members to be present and catch up on the latest news of the Society.

POLISH FALCONS OF AMERICA
2013 St. Louis Ave, 63106; (314) 921-1192.

The Polish Falcons of America, established in Chicago in 1887, was modeled after an organiztaion initiated in Poland. This fraternal organization, now counting 141 Nests in the U.S., offers social and cultural programs to its members and places great emphasis upon improving their physical and mental well-being, firmly believing in the tenet that within a healthy body lies a healthy mind. Biennial competitions are held in various districts and at the National Convention. National Folk dancing competitions are also held throughout the country. The PFA semi-annual newspaper keeps its members abreast of the news across the country. Visitors are welcome to all activities of the PFA Society, including the Polish Festival held annually the 1st week-end of Sept.

ST. LOUIS CENTER FOR INTERNATIONAL RELATIONS
5600 Lindell at Union, 63112; (314) 454-1744.

The St. Louis Center for International Relations is a not-for-profit organization created to foster awareness among St. Louisans of the benefits of interacting with the peoples and cultures of other nations. The Center strives to enhance the city's international profile and character and to stimulate international business, trade, education, and culture. Acting under the direction of the Mayor's office, the Center serves as primary liaison for the city's international relations and functions. It hosts visiting delegations, organizes mayoral delegations abroad, initiates special projects and events involving the city's major institutions, and acts as a clearing house for information and international protocol. In addition, the St. Louis Sister Cities program is a component of the Center's international project. St. Louis enjoys affiliations with 7 sister cities; Bologna, Italy; Galway, Ireland; Georgetown, Guyana; Lyon, France; Nanjing, China; Stuttgart, Germany; and Suwa, Japan. The Center is supporting initiatives to explore affiliations with cities in Eastern Europe, Latin America, and Africa. The creation and development of active exchanges are primarily the responsibility of the citizens who comprise the committees pursuing each affiliation. These relationships, in turn, obtain official recognition and proclamation through the mayors and governing bodies of respective cities. Among the other functions of the St. Louis Center for International Relations are the publication of a quarterly newsletter, *International Exchange,* a monthly calendar of International events in St. Louis, a guide for international living in the city, and a directory of local and regional organizations with an international focus in the arts, education, commerce, and ethnic cultures.

ST. LOUIS IRISH ARTS
7480 Whitehaven Dr, 63123; (314) 849-1662.

St. Louis Irish Arts, established in St. Louis in 1971, is a branch of the world-wide Comhaltas Ceoltoiri Eireann Society, whose goal is to preserve the Irish cultural heritage through teaching the Gaelic language and traditional Irish music, songs, and dances. The Society, also engaged in charitable programs, helps new immigrants adapt and establish themselves in their new lives. Lectures and other events are part of their programs at the local, national, and international levels. Their "Feis", an annual festival usually held in the 3rd week of Feb, provides St. Louis with a unique social experience.

SOCIEDAD HISPANO-AMERICANA OF ST. LOUIS
2300 Fairoyal Dr, 63131; (314) 822-0412 or 725-7065.

Sociedad Hispano-Americana of St. Louis, the oldest Hispano-American group in St. Louis, was established after World War II for the purpose of conversing in Spanish. English-speaking people began to join in 1955 and the Society became officially established as the Sociedad Hispano-Americana of St. Louis. This non-political organization promotes friendship, culture, and charity, and offers many programs. Their annual event is Pan-American Day held in Apr.

SWEDISH COUNCIL OF ST. LOUIS, INC.
400 Tamarack Dr, Ballwin, MO, 63011; (314) 389-6858.

The Swedish Council of St. Louis, an affiliate of the Swedish Council of America, was established in St. Louis in 1976 to promote knowledge and understanding of the Swedish heritage. The SCSL sponsors social, educational, and cultural events. Some annual activities are: The Valborgmassoafton, in Apr; the Midsommarfest, in May; a Smorgasbord in commemoration of Swedish King Gustavus II Adolphus, in Nov; and The Sankta Lucia Festival, held on or about Dec 13th.

56

57

58

59

FESTIVALS

St. Louis is a place of many interests, where life itself is reason enough for celebration. Annual festivals are listed below; for other events, check the Calendar sections of the Post-Dispatch and The Riverfront Times.

JANUARY

TRADITIONAL FETES DES ROIS, 1st week; (314) 432-0734.

MARTIN LUTHER KING CELEBRATION, 2nd week; (314) 533-3366.

ANNUAL ORCHID SHOW, Missouri Botanical Garden, 2nd or 3rd week; (314) 577-5100.

AUSTRALIA DAY, Jan 26; (314) 342-1649.

CHINESE NEW YEAR FESTIVAL, usually held between the last week of Jan and 3rd week of Feb; (314) 567-5540.

EAGLE DAYS, Clarksville, MO, 4th week-end; (314) 242-9662.

FEBRUARY

BALD EAGLE WATCH, Pere Marquette State Park Visitors Center, Grafton, IL, 1st week, (9am-Noon); (618) 786-2204 or 786-3323.

BLACK HISTORY MONTH, many events around town; check newspapers.

FETE DU BON VIEUX TEMPS, Cahokia Courthouse and Jarrot Mansion State Historic Sites, 107 Elm St, Cahokia, IL. Festival of the "good old days" held S before Ash W, 4-8pm. This festival celebrates the French colonial heritage of southwestern Illinois; (618) 332-1782.

FEIS FESTIVAL, Irish celebration, 3rd week; (314) 849-1662.

THE FASCHING BALL, Hermann, MO; (314) 486-2744.

MID-WINTER BENEFIT DANCE, American-Indian celebration, 3rd S, at Jefferson Barracks Park; (314) 351-0669.

MARDI GRAS CARNIVAL PARTY: (314) 966-0401.

MARCH

THE COUNTRY PEDDLER SHOW, Convention Center, Fifth St, St. Charles, MO, 1st week-end; (314) 946-7776.

ST. PATRICK'S DAY PARADES; (314) 776-9090 and check the Calendar sections of the Post-Dispatch and The Riverfront Times.

EQUINOX SUNRISE CEREMONY, Cahokia Mounds Historic Site, Cahokia, IL, Su closest to Mar 21; (618) 346-5160.

THE WURSTFEST, Hermann, MO, 3rd week-end; (314) 486-2744.

HOLI FESTIVAL, India's Spring Festival late Mar-Apr; (314) 432-5888 or 892-5991.

APRIL

EASTER EGG DISPLAY, National Shrine of Our Lady of the Snows, Belleville, IL; (618) 397-6700.

QUEEN'S BIRTHDAY CELEBRATION, Apr 7; (314) 962-2730.

PAN-AMERICAN DAY; (314) 822-0412 or 725-7065.

VALBORGMASSOAFTON; (314) 389-6858.

MAY

ST. LOUIS STORY TELLING FESTIVAL, Gateway Arch and Old Courthouse, 1st week-end; (314) 425-4465.

ASIAN PACIFIC AMERICAN HERITAGE MONTH; for listings of events call (314) 567-5540 or Coalition of Asian Americans.

CINCO DE MAYO, BATTLE OF PUEBLA CELEBRATION, May 5; (314) 739-2243.

ANNUAL VALLEY OF FLOWERS FESTIVAL, Florissant, MO, 1st week-end; (314) 837-0033.

LAUMEIER CONTEMPORARY ART AND CRAFT FAIR, Laumeier Sculpture Park, Geyer and Rott Rds, 2nd week-end; (314) 821-1209.

THE LEWIS AND CLARK RENDEZ-VOUS, Main St, St. Charles, MO, 3rd week-end; (314) 946-7776.

AMERICAN INDIAN DAY, Jefferson Barracks Historic Park, 3rd week-end; (314) 351-0669.

KIDS' DAY, Cahokia Mounds Historic Site, Cahokia, IL, 3rd Su of month; (618) 346-5160.

MAIFEST, Hermann, MO, 3rd week-end; (314) 486-2744.

ANNUAL INDIAN POW WOW FESTIVAL, Rockome Gardens, Arcola, IL, Memorial Day week-end; (217) 268-4216.

INTERNATIONAL FOLKLORE FESTIVAL, end of May and beginning of Jun; (314) 997-1445 or 921-1192.

MIDSOMMARFEST; (314) 389-6858.

VINTAGE AND AIRCRAFT DAYS FESTIVAL, St. Louis Aviation Museum, Spirit of St. Louis Airport, last week-end; (314) 524-1559.

ANNUAL MEMORIAL DAY RIVERBOAT RACE, St. Louis Riverfront, Memorial Day; (314) 421-1023.

GREEK MAY FESTIVAL; (314) 966-2255.

JUNE

BISSELL COUNTRY CRAFT FAIR, 10225 Bellefontaine, 1st week-end; (314) 889-3356.

RAGTIME RENDEZ-VOUS, 2nd week-end; (314) 533-1003.

MUSIC ON THE MISSOURI, Riverfront, St. Charles, MO, 3rd Su; (314) 946-7776.

CLASSIC DRAG BOAT RACES, Creve Coeur Lake, Dorsett and Marine, 2nd week-end; (314) 832-0200.

SUMMER SOLSTICE AT WOODHENGE, Cahokia Mounds Historic Site, Cahokia, IL, Su closest to Jun 21; (618) 346-5160.

ANNUAL ANTIQUE MARKET, Hermann, MO, 3rd week-end; (314) 428-2744.

SKT HANSAFTEN CELEBRATION, a Danish celebration of the Summer solstice, Jun 23; (314) 962-2730.

JULY

VP FAIR, Arch Grounds, Jun 30-Jul 4; (314) 535-FAIR.

ANNUAL ROCKOME GARDENS QUILT SHOW, Arcola, IL, 1st through 3rd week; (217) 268-4216.

THE RIVERFEST, Riverfront, St. Charles, MO, Jul 1-4th; (314) 946-7776.

SOULARD BASTILLE DAY, Soulard Neighborhood, Jul 14th; (314) 436-0828.

THE ANNUAL CLASSIC AEROPLANE RENDEZVOUS; (314) 434-3368.

COLOMBIA INDEPENDENCE DAY CELEBRATION, weekend following Jul 20th; (314) 567-4762.

JAZZFEST FESTIVAL, St. Charles, MO, 3rd week-end; (314) 946-7776.

PERU INDEPENDENCE DAY CELEBRATION, week-end following Jul 28th; (314) 966-0401.

ST. LOUIS STRASSENFEST, the annual German festival, 3rd week-end; (314) 721-7454.

AUGUST

THE GREAT STONE HILL GRAPE STOMP, Hermann, MO, 2nd Su; (314) 428-2744.

KIDS' DAY, Rockome Gardens, Arcola, IL, 1st week; (217) 268-4216.

THE ITALIAN FESTIVAL, at St. Ambrose Church, 5120 Wilson Ave, 2nd week-end; (314) 771-1228.

MELA FESTIVAL, Festival of India, 2nd week; (314) 432-6888 or 892-5991.

MEXICAN SOCIETY OF BENITO JUAREZ ANNUAL DANCE, 2nd week; (314) 739-2243.

ST. LOUIS CATHEDRALFETE, Lindell and Newstead, 3rd or 4th week-end; (314) 533-2824.

FESTIVAL OF THE LITTLE HILLS, Main St, St. Charles, MO, 3rd week-end; (314) 946-7776.

JEWISH FOLKLORE FESTIVAL, late summer; (314) 432-5700.

JAPANESE FESTIVAL, Missouri Botanical Garden, last week of Aug; (314) 577-5125.

SEPTEMBER

THE GREEK FESTIVAL, at St. Nicholas Greek Orthodox Church, 4967 Forest Park, Labor Day week-end; (314) 361-8925.

THE POLISH FESTIVAL, at 2013 St. Louis Ave (F and S after Labor Day); (314) 921-1192 or 868-4002.

THE JEWISH FOLK ART FESTIVAL, 2 Millstone Campus Dr, 1st week-end; (314) 432-5700.

GREAT FOREST PARK BALLOON RACE, at Forest Park, Lindell and Skinker, 2nd week-end; (314) 454-1488.

MEXICO INDEPENDENCE DAY, Sept 15th; (314) 739-2243.

BLUEGRASS FESTIVAL, Main St, St. Charles, MO, 2nd week-end; (314) 946-7776.

ARCOLA BROOM CORN FESTIVAL, Arcola, IL, 2nd week; (217) 268-4530.

ANNUAL COUNTRY FAIR, Six Flags; (314) 938-5300.

CIVIL WAR LIVING HISTORY, Main St, St. Charles, MO, 3rd week-end; (314) 946-7776.

THE VOLKSMARCH, Hermann, MO, 3rd week-end; (314) 428-2744.

DOG DAYS, The Dog Museum, Queeny Park, 1721 S. Mason Rd, 3rd week-end; (314) 821-DOGS.

THE HANLEY HOUSE FALL FESTIVAL, 7600 Westmoreland, 3rd week-end; (314) 727-8100.

TILLES PARK FALL ARTS AND CRAFTS FAIR, Litzinger and McKnight Rds, mid-Sept; (314) 889-2863.

ST. LOUIS NATIONAL CHARITY HORSE SHOW, at Queeny

Park, 550 Weidman Rd, 3rd week-end; (314) 391-0900.

SOLSTICE/EQUINOX SUNRISE AT WOODHENGE, Cahokia Mounds Historic Site, Cahokia, IL, Su closest to Sept 21; (618) 346-5160.

AUSTRALIA WEEK, Last of Sept-beginning Oct; (314) 342-1649.

VINTAGE AND AIRCRAFT DAYS FESTIVAL, St. Louis Aviation Museum, Spirit of St. Louis Airport, last week-end of Sept; (314) 524-1559.

HERITAGE AMERICA FESTIVAL, 4th week-end, Cahokia Mounds Historic Site, Cahokia, IL; (314) 351-0669 or (618) 346-5160.

OCTOBER

THE FAUST FOLK FESTIVAL, Faust Park, 1st week-end; (314) 532-7298.

OKTOBERFEST, Main St, St. Charles, MO, 1st week-end; (314) 946-7776.

THE APPLEFEST FESTIVAL, Clarksville, MO, 2nd week-end; (314) 242-3336 or 242-9683.

FRIENDSHIP LUNCHEON, PERUVIAN SOCIETY; (314) 966-0401.

OCTOBERFEST, Hermann, MO, every week-end in Oct; (314) 428-2744.

NOVEMBER

GATEWAY JAZZ FESTIVAL, Nov 1, 2, and 3; (314) 383-2633.

THE COUNTRY PEDDLER SHOW, Convention Center, Fifth St, St. Charles, MO, 1st week-end; (314) 946-7776.

THE ANNUAL JEWISH BOOK FESTIVAL, 2 Millstone Campus Dr, 63146, 1st week of Nov, and lasts 10 days, during which 25 renowned speakers and writers are featured; (314) 432-5700.

DEEPAWALI FESTIVAL, India Festival of Lights, 2nd or 3rd week; (314) 432-6888 or 892-5991.

THE ANNUAL FLORISSANT BY CANDLELIGHT HOUSE TOUR, Florissant, MO, 3rd week; (314) 837-3903.

ASHA PREM DANCES OF INDIA ANNUAL CONCERT; (314) 997-0911.

SMORGASBORD (Swedish); (314) 389-6858.

THE ANNUAL HAFLI, 931 Lebanon Dr, St. Raymond's Cedars Hospitality Room, week-end following Nov 16th; (314) 621-0056.

CHRISTMAS TRADITIONS, Main St, St. Charles, MO, from Thanksgiving to Dec 25; (314) 946-7776.

DECEMBER

LAUMEIER "FIRE AND ICE" SHOW, Laumeier Sculpture Park, mid-Dec; (314) 821-1209.

THE WAY OF LIGHTS, National Shrine of Our Lady of the Snows, Belleville, IL, 2nd week-Jan 8; (618) 397-6700.

AN OLD-FASHIONED CHRISTMAS, Hermann, MO; (314) 428-2744.

SWEDISH SANKTA LUCIA FESTIVAL, Missouri Botanical Garden, week-end following Dec 13th; (314) 389-6858.

CHRISTMAS CANDLELIGHT HOUSE TOURS, AND OTHER HOLIDAY EVENTS offered by most historic homes:

General Daniel Bissell House [99]	(314) 868-0973
Campbell House [30]	(314) 421-0325
Chatillon-De Menil Mansion [36]	(314) 771-5828
Eugene Field House and Toy Museum [32]	(314) 421-4689
Hanley House [75]	(314) 725-9155
Hawken House [49]	(314) 968-1857
Myers House [97]	(314) 921-4606
Oakland House [50]	(314) 352-5654
Payne-Gentry House [94]	(314) 739-5703
Sappington House [48]	(314) 966-4700
Shaw's House [39]	(314) 577-5150
Taille de Noyer [98]	(314) 524-1100
Thornhill [85]	(314) 532-7298
Wilson Price Hunt House [89]	(314) 383-7937

PERFORMING ARTS

AMERICAN THEATRE
*9th and St. Charles, 63101. A traditional theatre and a nightclub.
Cabaret/nightclub setting; (314) 231-7000.*

ASHA PREM DANCES OF INDIA
(314) 997-0911.

105 BLACK REPERTORY COMPANY
*2240 St. Louis Ave, 63106; Box office: 634 N. Grand, 10th Fl, Suite
F, 63103; (314) 534-3807.*

74 CENTER OF CONTEMPORARY ARTS — COCA
524 Trinity Ave, 63130; (314) 725-6555.

DANCE ST. LOUIS
149 Edgar Rd, 63119; (314) 968-4341.

EDISON THEATRE
*At Washington University, Forsyth Ave, Mallinckrodt Center,
63130; (314) 889-6543.*

54 FABULOUS FOX THEATRE
527 N. Grand, 63103; (314) 534-1678; ticket office: (314) 534-1111.

**KATHRINE DUNHAM CENTER FOR THE PERFORMING
ARTS**
*Southern Illinois University, 411 East Broadway, East St. Louis,
IL, 63201; (618) 482-6933; and Southern Illinois University at
Edwardsville; (618) 692-2000.*

65 THE MUNY
Forest Park, 63112; (314) 361-1900; ticket office: (314) 534-1111.

OPERA THEATRE OF SAINT LOUIS
Loretto Hilton Center, 139 Edgar Rd, 63119; (314) 961-0171.

REPERTORY THEATRE OF ST. LOUIS
130 Edgar Rd, 63119; (314) 968-4925.

81 ST. LOUIS COUNTY POPS
*Greensfelder Recreation Center, Queeny Park, 550 Weidman Rd,
Ballwin, 63011; Box office: (314) 534-1700.*

57 ST. LOUIS SYMPHONY ORCHESTRA
*Powell Symphony Hall, 718 N. Grand Blvd, 63103; Box office:
(314) 534-1700.*

73 ST. LOUIS CONSERVATORY AND SCHOOLS FOR
THE ARTS — CASA
560 Trinity Ave at Delmar, 63130; (314) 863-3033.

THEATRE PROJECT COMPANY
*New City School, 5209 Waterman Ave, 63108; Box office at 634 N.
Grand, Suite 10 H, 63103; (314) 531-1301.*

WEST PORT PLAYHOUSE
600 West Port Plaza, 63141; (314) 275-8787.

MAJOR SHOPPING MALLS

DOWNTOWN
ST. LOUIS CENTRE, 6th to 7th, Washington to Locust.
ST. LOUIS UNION STATION, at 1820 Market St.

SOUTH ST. LOUIS
CRESTWOOD PLAZA, 9501 Watson and Sappington Rds.

SOUTH COUNTY
SOUTH COUNTY SHOPPING MALL, Lindbergh Blvd and
Union Rd at Lemay Ferry Rd.

CENTRAL WEST END
MARYLAND PLAZA area, Euclid to Kingshighway, Lindell to
Delmar.

CLAYTON
ST. LOUIS GALLERIA, Clayton Rd and Brentwood.
PLAZA FRONTENAC, Clayton Rd and Lindbergh.

WEST COUNTY
CHESTERFIELD MALL, I-64 at Clarkson Rd.
WEST PORT PLAZA, I-270 at Page.
WEST COUNTY SHOPPING CENTER, I-270 at Manchester.

NORTH ST. LOUIS COUNTY
NORTHWEST PLAZA, at St. Charles Rock Rd and Lindbergh.
NORTHLAND, Lucas and Hunt Rd at W. Florissant.
JAMESTOWN MALL, Lindbergh Blvd at Old Jamestown Rd.
RIVER ROADS MALL, Jennings Station and New Halls Ferry.

ST. CHARLES
BOGEY HILLS PLAZA, Zumbehl and I-70.
MARK TWAIN MALL, 1355 S. Fifth.

ST. PETERS
MID-RIVERS MALL, I-70 and Mid Rivers Dr.

FAIRVIEW HEIGHTS, IL
ST. CLAIR SQUARE, 134 St. Clair Square. Access: I-64 to I-159.

ALTON, IL
ALTON SQUARE MALL, 200 Alton Square at Route 3.

ANTIQUE ROWS

SOUTH ST. LOUIS: Cherokee Antique Row, 52 antique shops, from 1700-2300 Cherokee St. For information and hours, Cherokee Antique Row Association, (314) 772-9177 or 773-8810.

CENTRAL WEST END: on Euclid Ave from Delmar to Lindell Blvd, McPherson Ave and Maryland Ave.

ST. CHARLES, MO, on Main St, and more from 806-1701 N. 2nd St. For information regarding St. Charles Antique Dealers, (314) 946-7776 or 1-800-366-2427.

ALTON'S ANTIQUE DISTRICT, 50 Antique Shops on Broadway from No. 9 to 1800. For information, Alton Antique Dealers' Association, (618) 462-1337.

GRAFTON ANTIQUE DEALERS on Main St, Grafton IL.

KIMMSWICK ANTIQUE DEALERS, along Main St, Kimmswick, MO.

ART GALLERIES

The large number of galleries in the area reflects the wide interest St. Louisans have for art. Barely scratching the available diversity, only a few have been listed here. Information regarding current exhibits are listed in the St. Louis Gallery Guide, available at all galleries. For more information, call The St. Louis Gallery Association at (314) 768-2626.

DOWNTOWN

ATRIUM GALLERY, Old Post Office; 815 Olive, 63101; (314) 621-1066. Contemporary art.

THE FORUM, 555 Washington, 63101; (314) 421-3791. Exhibits which address contemporary and historical issues.

SOUTH ST. LOUIS

AUSTRAL GALLERY, 2115 Park Ave, 63104; (314) 776-0300. Located in Historic Lafayette Square, brings to St. Louis the work of Australian artists, including exhibits of contemporary Aboriginal art.

GALLERY IN MOTION, 2928 Wisconsin Ave, 62118; (314) 772-0820. Animation art.

MIDTOWN

CUPPLES HOUSE AND McNAMEE ART GALLERY, 367. W. Pine Blvd, 63108; (314) 658-3025. Exhibits of St. Louis University's collection and local artists.

INTERWOVEN DESIGNS FIBERART GALLERY, 4400 Laclede at Newstead, 63108; (314) 531-6200. Contemporary fiber ar pieces including tapestries, hand-cast paper, and sculptures, as wel as unique wearable art pieces.

CENTRAL WEST END

MARTIN SCHWEIG GALLERY, 4648 Maryland, 63108; (314 361-3000. Photography exhibits.

UNIVERSITY CITY

COYOTE'S PAW, 6388 Delmar, 63130; (314) 721-7576. International art and crafts.

CRAFT ALLIANCE, 6640 Delmar, 63130; (314) 725-1151. Glass ceramics, wood, fiber, and jewelry art.

COMPONERE, 6509 Delmar, 63130; (314) 721-1181. Multimedia painting, art, furniture, and jewelry.

LITHOS GALLERY, 6301b Delmar, 63130; (314) 862-0674 African-American, Jamaican, and Haitian art.

CLAYTON

BARUCCI GALLERY, 8121 Maryland, 63105; (314) 727-2020 Regional and national art exchibits.

ETHICAL SOCIETY, 9001 Clayton Rd, 63117; (314) 991-0955. Local artists.

GOMES GALLERY, 8001 Forsyth, 63105; (314) 725-1808. Specializing in Southwestern art, including Native American artists. Unique Indian jewelry, pottery, sculpture, and weavings.

PHILLIP SAMUELS FINE ART, 8112 Maryland Ave, 63105; (314) 727-2444. By appointment only. This is the home of Ernest Trova's and Michael Rubin's work. The stark simplicity of this gallery offers a contemplative window on the contemporary American masters and sculptors.

THE SAINT LOUIS ART MUSEUM, Art Hill, Forest Park, 63110; (314) 721-0067. Ancient and Contemporary art. Asian, Renaissance, Impressionist, and American art. Exceptional Pre-Columbian collection.

WASHINGTON UNIVERSITY GALLERY OF ART, 1 Brookings Dr, 63110; (314) 889-5490 or (314) 889-4523. Exhibits of University's collection and student and faculty shows.

WEST COUNTY

MARIANIST GALLERY, 1256 Maryhurst, 63122; (314) 965-0877. Metal sculptures.

NORTH COUNTY

GARRETT GALLERY, 7717 Natural Bridge, 63121; (314) 381-3022. Local artists' exhibits and workshop.

ST. CHARLES

ARTIST GUILD, 524 S. Main St, 63301; (314) 733-8009.

ALTON, IL

TOWATA GALLERY AND STUDIOS, 206 W. Third St, 62002; (314) 726-1170. Sculpture and photographs of local, national contemporary artists.

EXCURSIONS

SEEING THE RIVER BY CAR
Driving through the city and immediate outskirts, the Mississippi, Missouri, and the Illinois can be seen from various spots:
* *The Mississippi:* downtown by the Gateway Arch [7]; at Jefferson Barracks Historical Park [43]; North Riverfront Park [100]; Alton [129] from Hwy 100, the Great River Road, a beautiful ride where the highway parallels the Mississippi River from Alton, IL, to Grafton [132] for 25 miles; Portage des Sioux.
* *The Missouri River:* at Frontier Park, St. Charles, MO [106].
* *The Illinois River:* from Grafton to Pere Marquette State Park [133], picturesque Hwy 100 is bordered by high bluffs overlooking the river.

9 GATEWAY RIVERBOAT CRUISES
500 N. L.K. Sullivan Blvd, 63102; (314) 621-4040. Open all year, except Thanksgiving, Dec 25, and Jan 1. Admission fee.

Operated by the oldest river excursion company on the Mississippi, the Huck Finn, the Tom Sawyer, and the Becky Thatcher offer 1-hour narrated cruises of the historic St. Louis Riverfront with frequent departures every day, Mar 1-Jan 1. Dinner Dixieland cruises too! Below the Arch, the Belle of St. Louis, St. Louis' newest cruising riverboat, offers a 2-hour day trip, T-Su, and Moonlight Dinner Cruises W-Su. A wide variety of entertainment on board, live music, and great reviews. Fun for the whole family.

10 FOSTAIRE HELIPORT

400 L.K. Sullivan Blvd, 63102; (314) 421-5440 or 421-3388 for information regarding tours of 10, 22, or 45 miles. Open every day, 10am-6pm, mid-Apr through Oct. Flights daily, 10am-dusk, depending on weather conditions.

An FAA-approved heliport, moored on the levee, offers tours of various lengths. Excellent for photography; a wonderful and quick way to see the city.

GRAY LINE SIGHTSEEING TOURS

P.O. Box 400, Caseyville, IL, 62232; (314) 241-1224. Everyday, 2-5pm, Apr through Oct. Reservations required.

3-hour tours in comfort to get a general idea of the highlights of the city without the driving. Bus pick up at all downtown hotels.

HORSE-DRAWN CARRIAGES

● BROOKDALE CARRIAGE CO
  2330 Osenfort, Glencoe, MO, 63038; (314) 458-0271.

● CHESHIRE CARRIAGE SERVICE; 647-7300.
  Enjoy an old-fashioned ride in a carriage downtown, in Forest Park, and Clayton. Horse-drawn rides for parties of 1 to 6, or ride to the Muny Opera in the "Hello Dolly" trolley car carriage pulled by 3 percherons. The coach can accommodate a party of 42 and leaves Cheshire Restaurant parking lot every nite at 7:30 during the Muny Opera season.

● ST. LOUIS CARRIAGE CO
  200 Chouteau, 63102; (314) 621-3334.
  Carriages are available daily after 6pm in front of the Adam's Mark Hotel on 4th St and in front of the Old Spaghetti Factory at 727 N. First St (Laclede's Landing), all year round.
  Rides downtown or through the park are offered until 2am. How long has it been since you've really had a quiet evening? Not only is this a fine way to enjoy the cool of the evening, but also the best time to take time for yourself and "really see" this city. The slow cloppety-clop cadence of the carriage will rock you, relax you, renew you, and remind you to slow down and experience life...

BALLOON EXCURSIONS
PARA-BALLOON ASSOC, INC
8920 Manchester, 63144; (314) BALLOON or 961-8929.
Week-end flights all year round. Daily flights from May through Oct. Time: at sunrise or 2 hours before sunset. Rides last 1 to 1½ hours. Call for prices.

Experience the thrill of a hot-air balloon ride in America's largest commercial balloon and see the world from a different perspective! These colorful hot-air balloons, still the only means available to fly at low altitudes, will allow you to see some of the most scenic parts of this area in about an hour and take spectacular photographs. The balloons vary in size, and the number of passengers determines the size of balloon used. There are balloons for "Couples Only" or America's largest certified passenger balloon, designed to accommodate 12 adults comfortably. At the landing site, following balloonists' tradition, champagne and Flight Certificate awarding ceremonies are conducted. Many additional features, such as an elegant after-flight gourmet dinner at the landing site, limousine service, video recording of the flight, strolling minstrels, etc., are available.

THE LEVEE LINE
707 N. 1st St, 63102; (314) 231-2345 in MO, and 1-800-2283-BUS in IL.

Operates 7 days a week from 10:50am-9:30pm, May through Dec. Bus can be taken from any bus stop along the downtown route.

The Levee Line busses (red, white, and blue) provide free transportation in the downtown area from Union Station to the St. Louis Centre, the Riverfront, and Laclede's Landing. (see map, page 131.)

evee Line

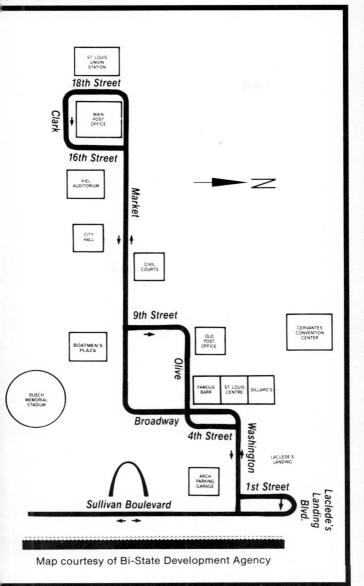

Map courtesy of Bi-State Development Agency

TOUR ST. LOUIS
6th and Cerre St, 63102; (314) 241-1400.
Operates 7 days a week, all year, 9am-4pm. Fee. Open-air trams Apr through Nov and enclosed vehicles the rest of the year.

Pick up available at all hotels of the St. Louis area. Narrated tours include the downtown and suburban areas, a 1-hour visit at a site of interest, and time for lunch.

112 CRUISES ON THE MISSOURI RIVER — SPIRIT OF ST. CHARLES

First Capitol St at Frontier Park, St. Charles, MO, 63303; (314) 946-1000 or 1-800-332-3448. Sightseeing tours daily at 2, May-Sept; Apr and Oct, S and Su at 2pm.

Treat yourself to a tour on the Missouri River, or a Dinner Cruise, a Moonlight Cruise, a 2-day cruise on the nearby three rivers with a night's stay at the luxurious Pere Marquette lodge. Entertainment ranges from banjo playing to ragtime music, blues, and gospel music.

132 TWIN RIVERS CRUISE ON THE BELLE OF GRAFTON

501 E. Front St, Grafton, IL, 62037; (618) 786-2318. Open May 15-Nov 15. Cruises M-F, 2pm; S-Su, Noon, 2, 4pm; F, Moonlight Cruise, 8:30-11pm; S, Dinner Cruise, 7-10pm; Bar and snacks available. Occasionally live entertainment with Dinner Cruise.

Come aboard! The Belle of Grafton, a 65-foot paddlewheeler replica sails on spectacular sections of the Mississippi and Illinois Rivers bordered by towering bluffs. An impressive sight anytime, particularly when autumn leaves turn to red and gold.

IMPORTANT PHONE NUMBERS

EMERGENCY **911**
AAA Auto Club
    road service 523-7300
    travel service 523-7373
Airlines
    American 1-800-433-7300
    Continental 241-7205
    Delta 421-2600
    Northwest 1-800-225-2525
    Southwest 421-1221
    TWA 291-7500
    U.S. Air......................... 1-800-428-4322
    United 1-800-241-6522
Airport Limousine 429-4940
Amtrak Station 1-800-872-7245
Attorney General's office 444-6816
Auto rental
    Avis (downtown) 241-5780
    Avis (airport) 426-7766
    Budget 731-6000
    Hertz (downtown) 421-3131
    Hertz (airport) 426-7555
Bi-State Transit 231-2345
Bus terminal.............................. 231-7800
Convention and Visitors Commission 421-1023
Crisis information 569-2161
Directory assistance 1-411
Emergency 911
Foreign exchange:
    Mercantile Bank, 8th and Locust 425-2895
    Boatmen's Bank, Boatmen's Plaza 554-6000
Guides
    for the city and suburbs 428-5332
    for the Hill........................... 647-2042
    for the Hill........................... 773-8901
Highway Patrol 434-3344
Hospitals
    Barnes 362-5000
    Cardinal Glennon Children's 577-5600
    Children's Hospital 454-6000
    Christian Hospital Northeast 355-2300
    Christian Hospital Northwest 839-3800
    Deaconess 768-3000
    DePaul Hospital...................... 344-6000
    Incarnate Word 865-6500
    Jewish Hospital 454-7000

St. Louis Regional Medical Center 361-1212
St. Mary's Health Center 768-8000
St. John's Mercy Medical Center 569-6000
Immigration office 539-2532
Interpreters
    Arabic 752-5462
    Chinese 721-1685
    Danish 962-2730
    French 429-4194
    752-5462
    German 273-6315
    Indian................................. 432-6888
    Polish 921-1192
    Portuguese............................. 429-4194
    Spanish 878-6895
    822-0412
    725-7065
    644-6455
    Tagaloh 832-3492
Kiel events Hot-Line........................ 241-1010
Laclede's Landing events .... 821-4200, press 9604
Local News .... 821-4200, press 4444
Locksmith, 24 hours 352-8585
822-7300
428-8200
Movie listings .... 821-4200, press 3456
Movie reviews .... 821-4200, press 9010
Parks
    City.................................. 535-1503
    County................................ 889-2863
    State................................1-800-334-6946
Pharmacy 24 hours 351-2100
Poison-control.............................. 772-5200
Southwestern Bell 571-1400
Special events in St. Louis .... 821-4200, press 9601
    at Union Station .... 821-4200, press 9607
    at the Zoo .... 821-4200, press 9609
    in sports .... 821-4200, press 9608
    at theaters .... 821-4200, press 9602
    at the Arch .... 821-4200, press 9605
    at Forest Park................... 821-4200, press 9606
    at the Lake of the Ozarks .... 821-4200, press 9610
    in jazz......................... 821-4200, press 8050
    in classical music .... 821-4200, press 8040
    in country music .... 821-4200, press 8026
    at local night clubs and dancing ..... 821-4200, press 8075
Sportsline-24 hrs scores and information 721-7200
321-1111

St. Louis Post-Dispatch 622-7000
Taxicabs
     Allen Cabs 241-7722
     Circle Cabs 521-6911
     Laclede Cabs 652-3456
     St. Louis County Cabs 991-5300
     Southwest Cabs 966-8294
     Yellow Cabs 361-2345
Temperature 321-2522
The Riverfront Times 231-6666
Time . . . . 821-4200, press 4010
Tourist Information Centers:
     for MO 869-7100
     for IL 1-800-ALTONIL
     for Southwestern IL 1-800-782-9587
Visitors Centers:
     St. Louis Visitors Center 241-1764
     St. Charles Visitors Bureau 946-7776
                                  1-800-366-2427
     Alton Visitors Center 1-800-ALTONIL
     Hermann Visitors Center 486-2744
     Arcola Visitors Center 217-268-4530
Translating firm 725-9466
Weather . . . . 821-4200, press 4445
Western Union 421-3967
Zip codes 436-4454

ALPHABETICAL TABLE OF CONTENTS

137

138

PHOTO ACKNOWLEDGMENTS

COVER PHOTOS: Front by Nick Adams; Back by Jeanne-Marie Smith; (1) Courtesy of Mississippi River Trading Co; (2) Photo by tom nelson, cm; (3), (4) Courtesy of M.R.T.C.; (5) Photo by J-M S; (6) LACLEDE'S LANDING and (7) THE OLD CATHEDRAL and (8) ST. LOUIS CITY HALL and (9) THE OLD COURTHOUSE and (10) EADS BRIDGE photos by J-M S; (11) MILLES FOUNTAIN and (12) THE OLD COURTHOUSE courtesy of M.R.T.C.; (13) UNION STATION photo by J-M S; (14) and (15) UNION STATION courtesy of M.R.T.C.; (16) ANHEUSER-BUSCH courtesy of Anheuser-Busch; (17) "THE IMMI-GRANTS" photo by J-M S; (18) TOWER GROVE PARK courtesy of Tower Grove Park; (19) MISSOURI BOTANICAL GARDEN photo by Jack Jennings, courtesy of Missouri Botanical Garden; (20) MISSOURI BOTANICAL GARDEN photo by tom nelson, cm; (21) GOLDEN EAGLE RIVER MUSEUM and (22) WAINWRIGHT BUILDING TERRA COTTA and (23) MISSOURI BOTANICAL GARDEN and (24) MISSISSIPPI RIVER and (25) MISSOURI BOTANICAL GARDEN and (26) TOWER GROVE PARK and (27) GRANT'S FARM and (28) GOLDEN EAGLE RIVER MUSEUM photos by J-M S; (29) POWELL SYMPHONY HALL courtesy of St. Louis Symphony Orchestra; (30) FABULOUS FOX THEATRE and (31) CATHE-DRAL OF SAINT LOUIS courtesy of M.R.T.C.; (32) COMP-TON HEIGHTS WATER TOWER photo by J-M S; (33) THE PRIVATE PLACES courtesy of Central West End Association; (34) THE ST. LOUIS ZOO courtesy of The St. Louis Zoo; (35) ST. LOUIS SCIENCE CENTER courtesy of St. Louis Science Center; (36) THE SAINT LOUIS ART MUSEUM courtesy of the Saint Louis Art Museum; (37) WASHINGTON UNIVERSITY MED-ICAL CENTER photo by J-M S; (38) CUPPLES HOUSE AND McNAMEE ART GALLERY courtesy of St. Louis University; (39) LAUMEIER SCULPTURE PARK and (40) THE PRIVATE PLACES photos by J-M S; (41) LAMBERT-ST. LOUIS INTER-NATIONAL AIRPORT courtesy of Lambert-St. Louis Interna-tional Airport; (42) OAKLAND HOUSE and (43) SOULARD FARMER'S MARKET photos by J-M S; (44) and (45) LAMBERT-ST. LOUIS INTERNATIONAL AIRPORT MURALS and (46) WEST PORT PLAZA and (47) WASHING-TON UNIVERSITY and (48) CENTRAL WEST END photos by J-M S; (49) "MESA", LITHOGRAPH by R.C. GORMAN cour-tesy of Gomes Gallery; (50) Photo by John Phelan, courtesy of Interwoven Designs Fiberart Gallery; (51) "KURTAL", AUS-TRALIAN ABORIGINAL ART by JARINYANU DAVID DOWNS courtesy of Austral Gallery; (52) UNIVERSITY CITY LION GATES courtesy of University City's City Hall; (53) NATIONAL SHRINE OF OUR LADY OF THE SNOWS courtesy of National Shrine Of Our Lady Of The Snows; (54) THE ST. LOUIS BLUES photo copyright © 1990 Mark Buckner; (55) STUDY/FALLING MAN (WALKING JACKMAN) SCULPTURE by TROVA photo by J-M S; (56) SPIRIT OF ST CHARLES courtesy of M.R.T.C.; (57) PURINA FARMS courtesy of Purina Farms; (58) THE ST. LOUIS ZOO courtesy of The St. Louis Zoo; (59) SIX FLAGS OVER MID-AMERICA courtesy of Six Flags Over Mid-America; (60) MERAMEC CAVERNS photo by Art Grossman courtesy of Meramec Caverns; (61) CAHOKIA MOUNDS HISTORICAL SITE courtesy of Cahokia Mounds Historical Site; (62) CLARKSVILLE SKYRIDE photo by Bruce Martin; (63) ROCKOME GARDENS courtesy of Rockome Gardens; (64) Photo by Tom Urban; (65), (66), (67), (68), (69) (70) Photos by J-M S.

64

65

66

67

68

69